The *Beautiful* Work

Contemplations On Why We Teach

Tim Joy

Principal, Director of Mission
De La Salle North Catholic High School
2010 – 2024

Fountain Pen Books
Milwaukie, Oregon

Library of Congress Control Number:
2025925287

ISBN (Paperback): 979-8-9939216-0-0

Printed in the United States of America
First Edition: 2026

The nine visitations into the life of John Baptist de La Salle
emerged from my imagination but are based
on historical events as depicted in multiple biographies
as well as De La Salle's letters and memoirs.

Unless specifically cited,
all images are from adobestock.com

Instagram @inkbytimjoy
Facebook.com/timjoy

Cover Design: River Design Books

Fountain Pen Books
Milwaukie, Oregon

DEDICATION

To my students and colleagues at
La Salle High School (1983 – 2003) and
De La Salle North Catholic High School (2002 – 2024)

⊕   ⊕   ⊕

"He that shall do and teach shall be called great in
the kingdom of heaven."

Matthew 5:19

A Teacher's Year

⊕ Visitations from John Baptist de La Salle's life

The Ceaseless Why

The frenetic maze of students clambering for the next class, the sobbing sophomore, clips of papers stuffed into a teacher's bag, a student slouched in the chair outside the Dean's office, a line of parents at conference night, the shades drawn in the Principal's office, a custodian driving the waxer down an empty hallway, students laughing at a lunch table, a teacher staying late with students, red flashes on the school's answering machine.

These scenes depict the mission landscape our staff navigates every day at De La Salle North Catholic High School in Portland, Oregon.

If you asked William Blake, he'd say the scenes are the portals to our place in the cosmos.

To see the world in a grain of sand and heaven in a wildflower.

If you asked Elizabeth Barrett Browning, she'd say they are the heaven crammed into our school community.

Earth is crammed with heaven, and every common bush afire with God.

If you asked Ralph Waldo Emerson, he'd say they are the facts of the spiritual field in which we work.

Prayer is the contemplation of the facts of life from the highest point of view.

If you asked Mary Oliver, she'd tell us to pay attention since each scene portrays our longing.

The real prayers are not the words, but the attention that comes first.

If you asked John Baptist de La Salle, he'd say these scenes reveal the path of our sacred purpose and salvation.

In the light of faith, you see things quite differently.

Of course, we rarely see it in any of those ways. In the rush-push of school life, we parcel the scenes to two lists on a t-graph: my-job and not-my-job; or we note it all peripherally, a blur as we hurry by to check off an item on our to-do list, likely the same list we carried yesterday.

This book tells stories from the dynamic panorama of school life, the whole year of it, the getting up each day, the walking into classrooms and offices, the never-ending, full-throttle, beautifully exhausting work of it all.

Tell your school's story

Over the last 100 years, staff compositions in Catholic schools have flipped. Whereas, once it was predominantly vowed religious men and women, it is now lay men and women who fill nearly all school positions. Whereas, once teachers lived together and near their school, now teachers live separate from colleagues and far from their school. These changes birthed a challenge for independent Catholic schools which profess a faith story about their founding, a particular way of living the Gospel message in their school. Whether Jesuit, Holy Names, Lasallian, or others, each society's spiritual legacy—its *charism*—should animate the communal life of its school.

How, then, do today's lay teachers embrace their school's charism?

It is to this question and to this vast group of heroically dedicated, lay faculty and staff that *The Beautiful Work* was written.

The short answer is, first, examine the "substance of daily experience...to see the gospel dimension of that service and all its demands";[1] and, second, share your story with colleagues. In modern parlance, sharing is how a "meme" takes hold. For Lasallian schools, our stories are about a community's faithful zeal for educating youth.

For that, we'll need to travel through time . . . back to 17th century Reims, France, where we meet a young priest named Frère De La Salle and see what he got himself into.

---

[1] Campos, Miguel, FSC. "Introduction." *Meditations for the Time of Retreat* by John Baptist de La Salle. Winona, MN: Saint Mary's College Press, 1975, pp 1-44.

St. John Baptist de La Salle, Patron Saint of Teachers

John Baptist de La Salle (1651–1719) was born into a wealthy and politically prominent family in Reims, France. From an early age, he was drawn to the priesthood and expected to fulfill his life's ministry within the incensed corridors of the Roman Catholic Church.

At least, that's how it started out.

However, within a month after his ordination in April 1678, the first fissures opened in that imagined life when the sudden death of a friend led him to take up his friend's work: help a community of Sisters run a free school for girls. Less than a year later, De La Salle found himself quietly helping a benefactor establish another free school, this time for boys. Five months later, a second school opened across town.

The hometown-priest thing was starting to get away from him.

By 1690, there were eight schools—two in Paris—and a growing society of teachers who called themselves "Brothers." By 1705, there were schools in 12 cities. At the time of De La Salle's death in 1719, there were about 100 Brothers serving in over 30 schools.

Today, De La Salle is widely regarded as an educational reformer: he pioneered simultaneous instruction; foreswore Latin so that students could develop mastery in French; provided pedagogical training to Brothers and established Teacher Colleges for aspiring lay teachers, the first of its kind in France. Along the way, he started a weekend school for working students and opened vocational schools that taught bookkeeping, accounting, and mechanics.[2]

Not everyone was happy about it. He frequently wrangled with teacher guilds, city councils, local pastors and prelates, all to ensure that the Brothers' schools remained independent, non-clerical, and free to all.

Centuries pass.

In May 1900, John Baptist de La Salle was canonized a saint; in May 1950, he was declared the Patron Saint of Teachers.

---

[2] *John Baptist De La Salle: the Founding Story of Lasallian Education.* The Brothers of the Christian Schools, District of San Francisco | New Orleans. Napa, CA: 2009.

As of 2025, there are about 3,000 Christian Brothers worldwide in association with 100,000 lay teachers and staff serving a million students in 1,100 schools located in 80 countries. Each school follows the traditions established by the Christian Brothers whose charism is to live by a Spirit of Faith and Zeal inspired by their Founder, St. John Baptist de La Salle. We call these schools *Lasallian*.

This book is about one of those schools.

De La Salle North Catholic High School in Portland, Oregon

De La Salle North Catholic High School is the most diverse private high school in Oregon. Its students enter high school about a grade and a half behind national norms in multiple disciplines. As a member of the Cristo Rey Network, the school contracts with local corporate partners and students work five days a month in those companies, earning roughly half the cost of their education as they also learn important life-long skills. Through this Corporate Work Study program, the school's rigorous curriculum, and the students' tenacious resolve, 98% of seniors, on average, earn acceptance to colleges and universities, an uninterrupted achievement since its first class graduated in 2005.

Like your own school, the faculty and staff at De La Salle North Catholic High School feel called to serve and do so with an uncommon zeal for young people. Since opening in 2001, the school's staff has faithfully carried out the Lasallian mission to serve the families and students in the Portland area by creating access to college and careers.

Working in a school calls upon one's moral core. Up close, the *always-on* needs of any school seem topsy-turvy and urgent. Over time's long arc, however, the work takes on a kind of grandeur.

In my tenure as Principal and later as Director of Mission, I walked the halls looking for the images and voices of our school. What I saw were the outward signs of our staff's inward grace, the daily emanations of the Lasallian charism of faith and zeal: trust in providence, fidelity to grace, and the great miracle—touching the hearts of students.

How this book came to be, and what's in here

On school-night Sundays from September 2010 to June 2024, I sat at my desk and composed vignettes about the daily life of our school, a weekly riff on the words of De La Salle. This helped me see that the plodding events of an ordinary school day were, in fact, scenes of faithful people working out their purpose and meaning, chaotic though it be, every pulse of it the outward sign of an inward ceaseless why.

The Beautiful Work is organized on the months of an academic year, each month containing four elements:
- Lasallian meme tied to a month's primary challenge
- Pivotal story in John Baptist de La Salle's life
- Series of Sunday night messages, dated and timestamped
- Reflection questions based on the month's meme

Consider September. The Lasallian meme is "know your students individually," since scant learning occurs unless there's a positive relationship between the student and the teacher. Next, an imaginative narrative depicts the teenage Jean-Baptiste in the De La Salle family home the night before he takes a big step toward priesthood. There follows a chronological sampling of Sunday night emails from the Septembers occurring between 2010 and 2023. The chapter concludes with reflection questions on September's meme.

And so it goes, September through May . . . one academic year in a school's work meandering amid the confluences of John Baptist de La Salle's life. It's about the steady ethos of one school following its north star so that young people might grow in wisdom and grace.

Tim Joy
Milwaukie, Oregon
December 2025

Prologue
see things quite differently

Prologue

"You are right in saying that in the light of faith, you see things quite differently from when they are looked at in themselves without going beyond the natural view.

St. John Baptist de La Salle – *Letter 118*[3]

There's a consciousness about the world that comes from being Catholic or working in a Catholic setting, especially in a school. James Joyce captures it this way: "In the particular is contained the universal." In the poetic realm, it's the mundane cracking a window on the transcendent. In a Catholic realm, it's a "sacramental consciousness."

There's always a deeper story in life than just what happens.

This is what De La Salle was getting at. If you work in a school, you must look at your work as *always signifying more than what you see.*

The Prologue email was sent the Sunday night before the second semester opened and posed De La Salle's question about this poetic, sacramental view:

Do you look upon your work in this way?

When you don't, the work can be a soulless slog. When you do, teaching is suffused with purpose and meaning.

⊕   ⊕   ⊕

---

[3] De La Salle, John Baptist. *The Letters of John Baptist de La Salle*. Romeoville, Ill., Lasallian Publications, 1988.

Jan 29 – Feb 2, 2024
1 message   Sun, Jan 28, 2024 at 7:48 PM

"With the eyes of faith, you see things quite differently."

St. John Baptist de La Salle
Letter #117, to a lay woman

About a block and a half from my house, Johnson Creek flows just beneath the 55th Street bridge, one I can walk under in the summer.

Today, it's 65° . . . 50 degrees warmer than it was two weeks ago . . . and the crocuses are up amid fall's faded leaves and winter's downed limbs.

The hard flow of a swollen creek and the bright hues of spring remind me that change is underway . . . is *always* underway. We tend to look at the world in a static, snapshot sort of way . . . one image at a time, everything stopped, captured, a false story of the pace and drama of actual living.

In another venue, standing in the hall during passing time, for instance, it's all a mashup of teen vitality. Consider the many other moments in a single day at De La Salle North Catholic: a freshman looks at the senior map of colleges, students eat lunch on a bench in the science wing, a pair of sophomores sit with a tutor in the Resource Center, 4th Period Leadership students converse in the Commons, the Chem teacher sits alone in the lab reading students reports, a counselor consoles a crying student in her office, and, after school, students in a classroom work problem sets.

Every day. One thing after another.

De La Salle called this "looking at things in themselves without going beyond the natural view." In his correspondence with a lay woman, De La Salle offered spiritual guidance about looking on the world with the eyes of faith, as one might see the world if fitted with a different lens . . . you see life's flow, perhaps as providential, moments imbued with a transcendence when you realize that what you are doing is more than a single thing at a single time, but acting out of a devout agency born of a desire to serve, to care. You have broken through, and suddenly you "see things quite differently." Suffused with purpose and meaning. Our ceaseless why.

Do you look at your work this way? When you do, that's when our school hums. It's palpable.

We come to this school to be part of the Lasallian community that serves here . . . and "to acquit ourselves of our work with zeal and unselfish generosity . . . [and] to maintain a union among ourselves" in that service.[4]

Bless you all in the ceaseless flow of beautiful work you carry out with care and love.

---

[4] The quoted lines are from De La Salle's final testament, the "last instructions and final directives" he gave to the Brothers.

September

know your students individually

September

"Know your students individually and be able to understand them."

St. John Baptist de La Salle – *Meditation 33.1*

In every genre of De La Salle's writing, be it *The Conduct of the Christian Schools,* or *Meditations for the Time of Retreat*, or his decades of letters to his fellow Brothers, De La Salle urged his teachers to know and understand the students confided to their care.

What is the origin of this insistent Lasallian meme?

This is why our first visitation from De La Salle's life occurs the night before he joins the Cathedral canonry at age 15. His siblings don't really understand what's about to happen. His mother is preoccupied with little Pierre, barely one; and, over dinner, his father asks again, "Are you sure about this?"

Wistful, De La Salle ponders this step now, how it looms larger than he first imagined.

This, then, is the first task of a Lasallian educator—discover your students, listen to their stories, and be curious about them. Every lesson you have planned for them, and every hope you nurture for them, depends on this first thing.

The De La Salle Family Home
Reims, France, January 6, 1667

On the eve of Jean-Baptiste de La Salle receiving his canonry (a Church position with Cathedral duties and benefits), he paces in his bedroom at the family home, about a block and a half behind the Cathedral of Notre-Dame of Reims. He wondered if his family understood his decision, why he wanted to be a canon and a priest. He was 15 years old.

The new year had opened cold and grey, winds sweeping in from the south. Rain yesterday and the day before. Rather colder tonight than last night. Out on the Rue de Marguerite, snow mixed in with the rain. In the waggling light of his bedside candle, the text of the canon's oath shook in Jean-Baptiste's hand; he steadied himself, wanting to speak the words evenly, calmly.

"I, Jean-Baptiste de La Salle, canon of this church of Reims, swear on the holy and divine Gospels that I will faithfully give advice as required and according to my conscience to my church at Reims."[5]

What was, a few weeks ago, a simple reading through lines was now like swallowing chalk. Father will be there. Mother. The family, grandma, *le mère*. Even so, as he whispered aloud "canon of this church of Reims," the words heaved in his lungs.

He swallowed. Started over. "I, Jean Baptiste de La Salle . . ."

His mind flew ahead, imagining the morrow, dressed in his cassock, knocking on the great canon portal and stepping into the chilled, incensed air of the cathedral, his family and professors gathered in the nave.

". . . according to my conscience to my church at Reims."

My conscience. He wondered what this might be, some wadded-up clamp of promises, and whether he could, over the years ahead, keep

---

[5] Canons have spoken this oath since 1259. Salm, Luke, FSC. *John Baptist de La Salle: The Formative Years*. Romeoville, Ill., Lasallian Publications, 1989.

such an oath. *Impossibles?*

The night had quieted his recitations as the cold deepened, and the rain slowly yielded its essence to mostly snow. Even with the windows pulled and closed tight, a gust pushed on the mullion, jittering the bolt in its clasp. Jean-Baptiste rose from his desk, tested the clasp, and looked out from his room, flung out over the street, where he viewed the cathedral's chevet and imagined tomorrow morning . . . the walk to the church, kneeling next to Frère de Vienne,[6] ready to be vested.

"We have voted to admit you into the canonry."

Images flooded his memory . . . running in the courtyard of his old home a few blocks away . . . summer, the cathedral towers stark against the blue sky . . . fall, the farmers' markets like a carnival, doused with the wash-over breezes of harvests up the valley . . . kneeling in the Archbishop's chapel as he received his tonsure . . . walking in the rain down the narrow Rue Vauthier-le-Noir and passing beneath the angel archway at the Collège[7] . . . sitting in class writing out tedious Latin declensions . . . memorizing Cicero's orations.

Before attending the Collège, he walked with his father to his office at the Court of Justice, sometimes holding his hand. It was secure and warm and certain. He wondered about his father's long silences over this last year. *Is he proud of me wanting to be a priest?*

Outside, it was a steady snowfall, gauzing his view of the Cathedral.

It had all happened so fast. He ran his hand over his tonsure, rubbed it, tapped it twice.

"*Demain*," he spoke aloud. Tomorrow.

After completing his studies at the Collège, Jean-Baptiste attends University of Reims for one year and then travels to Paris to attend Saint Sulpice Seminary and the Sorbonne in his second year.

---

[6] Father Louis de Vienne, provost, University of Reims.
[7] Collège des Bons Enfant, where De La Salle went to school as a young boy.

Sep 7 – 10, 2010

1 message   Mon, Sep 6, 2010 at 9:47 PM

"Do not doubt that God gave you a great gift - the grace to be a teacher to others."

St. John Baptist de La Salle
Meditations for the Time of Retreat, 9.1

So, we start.

For a few of us, September 7 marks the first day working in a school setting; for others, it's another First Day, when those light jitters in our stomach reveal a nutty excitement even after 15 or 20 or 25 years of teaching. It's in our blood, this work.

We come off a week and a half of preparation for this year. All of the individual and departmental work in Chicago preparing college-ready curricula, our math department off to Minneapolis to focus on method-ology, colleagues working on Masters degrees, staff reading in their field and about our students, teachers and administrators assisting with our largest summer school ever, the Corporate Work Study office training a record number of students, our Admissions staff working tenaciously to bring "capable, motivated and interested"[8] students to our care . . . all of this dynamic and sacred force moves toward one goal: preparing our students to be competent, faith-filled, college-ready citizens.

I am reminded of what many of our newest members said about this community last Thursday at noon: you are tremendously dedicated teachers and staff. Have no doubt that, together and with grace, we will accomplish our goals.

---

[8] This was a key phrase in the school's original Mission Statement of 2001.

Thank you to all for a fruitful summer and for your persistent passion for our students and this school.

Sep 6 – 9, 2011
1 message   Mon, Sep 5, 2011 at 8:24 PM

"Young people need good teachers, like visible angels."

St. John Baptist de La Salle
Meditations for the Time of Retreat, 5.1

Do you remember your first day of high school?

Now in 2011, all over Portland—and all over the United States—families finished the last touches this weekend on their preparations for school: purchasing pens and paper and pencils, ironing clothes, filling up backpacks, making sure the provisions are in order for a week's succession of lunches and snacks. Last week, yellow buses were out making practice runs. In thousands of schools, just as we have, staffs have prepared hallways and kitchens and classrooms.

What kind of space do we want our students to enter?

It's Labor Day evening, summer's last sunset, and it's a school night. Parents and students alike share some anxiety: who will be with my child during the day? Who

> *It's Labor Day evening, summer's last sunset, and it's a school night.*

will my teacher be? At our Lasallian school, De La Salle reminds us to take care with that real worry families harbor: we are to be guardian angels to our students. It's an archaic term, guardian angel, but apt—you are a protector. They may be teens and occasionally present a tough façade, but they are still children and need our careful, communal guidance. Let us all be visible, vigilant.

⊕   ⊕   ⊕

7

"You have been called by God to this ministry, and you have been given the grace of teaching and the gift of exhortation for the sake of those entrusted to your responsibility."

St. John Baptist de La Salle
Meditations for the Time of Retreat, 1.2

It's a school night.

Throughout Portland, families of De La Salle North Catholic students are preparing for Tuesday morning—the first day of school. For some families, it is the first day of their son's or daughter's senior year, a time thick with worry about academics and college applications. For still others, Tuesday marks the first day of a child in high school. We do have a sense of these pressures on families and their children, what they have come to hope for in us because they have chosen De La Salle North Catholic, where they will be "entrusted to [our] responsibility."

In my mind's eye, I see the throng push open the front doors on Tuesday morning and flow up the stairs, behind them a thousand invisible trails of worry and doubt and fear. I'll say, *Good Morning, Happy First Day, You Look Great,* and *So Good To See You.* Some will answer back, shout *Hello!* Some will go right by, on to First Period, those pressures flickering in their heads. In our hallways and cafeteria and counseling offices and classrooms, they will lean in just a bit, surreptitiously glad to see us all again.

Each moment is a sacred exchange within our ministries

They are here because you each have a grace and gift. Every moment with a child is a moment she or he may wonder if this

8

world can be trusted . . . each moment, then, is a sacred exchange within our ministries. And we can only fulfill the ministry to which we are called when we teach and exhort, wherever or however that occurs in our building. Our students need us.

Pray for the strength to carry out the work to which you are called.

"The children in your care are a letter which Christ dictates to you, which you write each day in their hearts, not with ink, but by the Spirit of God."

St. John Baptist de La Salle
Meditations for the Time of Retreat, 3.2

Huston Smith, author of international bestseller *The World's Religions* (1958), contends recently (*Why Religion Matters*, 2001) that modernity—things and knowledge—have edged out mystery and a yearning for the divine. However, he counters that "the finitude of mundane existence cannot satisfy the human heart completely." We long for the ineffable Other. Modernity, materialism, naturalism (name your -ism) may fascinate us, titillate us; but it cannot quell this longing; in fact, our modern times seem only to intensify our longing. And being unrequited, we tend toward alienation. Look around: Syria, Ukraine, Ferguson, name some more. It is easy to feel as if the social fabric frays at the touch.

Here at De La Salle North Catholic, our daily communal work of loving our students stirs this sense of belonging. Just as De La Salle instructed his young Brothers three centuries ago, we receive our students as if they were love letters dictated to us, but which we recompose in their hearts. Consequently, they belong, and we conduct this most precious mission. As each child enters our school, walks through the halls, enters a class-room or an office, talks to us at lunch, Christ's dictation comes to us; in this metaphor, every Child is the very Word of God. And so, for us, every gentle gesture, every true word, every correction done with love, every smile with a name called, is the letter we compose upon the hearts of our students.

Only in faith can we do this.

Sep 6 – 9, 2016

1 message   Mon, Sep 5, 2016 at 8:07 PM

"To be entrusted with the teaching of the young is a great gift and grace of God."

St. John Baptist de La Salle
Meditations for the Time of Retreat, 9.1

How do we look upon this work we do?

For De La Salle and his Brothers, teaching the young was their response to the soul-deep call from God, the way to their own salvation as well as the salvation of the students entrusted to them. It's a big ask, don't you think?

Friday, sophomores filled the auditorium to the corners. You know sophomores . . . 15-years-old, cooler than freshmen, more certain of their obvious coolness than even juniors, relatively convinced that their coolness will exceed that of some seniors when they are themselves seniors. (Let us remember . . . we all were them once.). They would not admit to any eagerness or pleasure in returning to school. But there they sat, nonetheless. Ahead, there will be spectacular days of exuberant learning; and there will be other kinds of days when what happens calls up other words.

It may be hard on such singular days to remember the long view . . . that our "great gift and grace" is that, with sophomores, we have three years to form them, prepare them, learn with them. In that way . . . in that *total experience over time* . . . there resides the reason we are here, why we are "entrusted with the teaching" of our beautiful students.

Dear Colleagues . . . I pray and hope that this is a week of great excitement with our students. Please take time to step outside your office or classroom in the morning, in the passing times, at lunch . . . and welcome our students to the 2016-2017 school year, one of the four years of high school they will remember a lifetime.

©Kara Arundel/K-12 Dive

Aug 28 – Sep 1, 2017
1 message   Sun, Aug 27, 2017 at 7:58 PM

"The Lasallian community today consists of a people who bind them-selves together in solidarity with others to ensure that the Christian school or Lasallian work in which they work will be a place of 'salvation' for all the young people who attend it."

Br. Gerard Rummery, FSC
From "Lasallian Spirituality"

Friday morning, the Class of 2021 gathered in Kenton Park with several staff to move through their first Lasallian retreat—a time to reflect on their transition from grade school into a new time of growth and challenges from which they will eventually emerge as young adults.

It was a beautiful day to be in the park.

The ninth graders were in small groups in the open area east of the ball fields, trying to figure out how to all stand on a sheet and simultaneously flip it over. There was lots of confusion. Some groups were bunched to one side of the sheet, others were still standing on the grass, with various people in the group pointing and talking at the same time. A few minutes went by, and one could see that light had dawned on a few groups and they were systematically working it out. There were, also, a couple of groups stuck; some frustration was evident.

In other words, the activity was working as designed. Team building is never a straight line. It is a working out of trust, of believing that a team can solve the problem it *Team building is never a straight line. It is a working out of trust.* faces, each team member laboring to do her part, yielding here, asserting there.

Even when a group knew how to stand on the sheet and turn it over, they still made mistakes, and so the group failed. They'd start over, knowing how to right the error. It was kind of wonderful to observe.

This week, we start year 17 for our beloved school, preparing ourselves as a community to serve the students "confided to our care." The quotation has a deep Lasallian tradition, a phrase that De La Salle himself used all through his meditations for his Brothers and in his personal letters to Brothers, friends, benefactors, and priests. As he would say, in the eyes of faith, God had chosen the Brothers and the students simultaneously. It was the calling of that community of Brothers to deduce the most efficacious methods of instruction for those students.

I really do believe that we can stand on a sheet and turn it over.

Sep 5 – 8, 2017
1 message   Mon, Sep 4, 2017 at 8:32 PM

On September 2, 2017, the Eagle Creek Fire erupted 25 miles east of Portland in the Columbia Gorge, ignited by fireworks tossed from a trail. Strong east winds pushed smoke and ash into the Portland metro area, cancelling numerous after-school activities, closing I-84, the Union Pacific railroad, and all ship traffic on the Columbia River. The fire burned 48,000 acres and was not contained until November 30.

"The greatest miracle you can perform is to touch the hearts of your students."

St. John Baptist de La Salle
Meditation 139.3 – Feast of St. Peter

What a strange evening this Monday has been. A dull red sun setting behind wildfire smoke and fine ash falling in parts of the city. I imagine many thousands of people throughout the state looking to the compass points to take in this oddity—how it is we had a winter that was the coldest and wettest in 20 years, and now the summer appears to be one of the driest and hottest on record. Makes me think about our school . . . and the great variability of our students through an academic year.

We are about to embark on the beautiful work. It's beautiful because it draws so much goodness out of you.

There will be times this year when you may question what you're doing, question the efficacy of your work, question if you are in the right place. There, you may face some dark times. De La Salle addressed such moments with zeal—pray for your students, pray for your Brothers. And then get back to work. As much as De La Salle was a faithful man, he was also a pragmatic one. With zeal, and faith, good things follow.

I have such faith in us as a community united in purpose—to touch the hearts and teach the minds of the students confided to us. *Confided—* given in faith. The families we serve believe in us. With such faith in us, how do we come to this work except with humility and compassion? We fall for our students, we love them . . . and that is why we push them. We see in them something they may not yet see themselves.

Sep 3 – 6, 2019
1 message   Mon, Sep 2, 2019 at 7:41 PM

"Second-mountain organizations touch people at their depths and leave a permanent mark. You always know when you meet a Marine, a Morehouse man, a Juilliard pianist, a NASA scientist. These institutions have a collective purpose, a shared set of rituals, a common origin story. They nurture thick relationships and demand full commitment. They don't merely educate, they transform."

David Brooks
The Second Mountain

What is the indelible mark, the lifetime ethos, that De La Salle North Catholic High School leaves with our students?

To David Brooks, those ascending a career's first mountain seek personal success and achievement; those ascending their second mountain seek things that matter "for the other."

Our Lasallian Catholic school enters its 19th year focused on building our communal capacity to live out De La Salle's vision of an education that touches hearts in order to "provide a human and Christian education, especially the poor." What is a human education but one that responds to the direct and immediate needs of the students in their care. The Brothers' schools taught in the French vernacular, eschewing Latin—much to the consternation of the local church authority—because it provided no advantage to their students; in fact, De La Salle considered Latin a hindrance to his pupils' education as it precluded practice in and, thereby, proficiency in French.

The students we serve enter De La Salle North Catholic with strengths and gifts sometimes obscured by test scores and inexperience with academic rigor, each with big hopes strained by circumstances out of their control. It is often the case that what our students need from us cannot be found on any academic standard or benchmark.

And so it comes to us—each of us—committed to our shared vision of our beloved Lasallian school . . . to be an older sister or brother to our students . . . and to be a sister and brother to each other.

As we are with each other, so we are to our students.

Sep 8 – 11, 2020
1 message   Mon, Sep 7, 2020 at 8:15 PM

Arid east winds from the upper Columbia Plateau funneled through the Columbia Gorge, overtopped sylvan reaches of the Cascade foothills and fanned devastating, record-breaking wildfires in Oregon and Washington in late August and early September 2020, putting some of our staff on evacuation alert. Add to this, the school year began under rigid COVID-19 protocols with all classes online.

"Union in a community is a precious gem, which is why the Lord so often recommended it to His disciples before He died. If we lose this, we lose everything. Preserve it with care, therefore, if you want your community to survive."

St. John Baptist de La Salle
Meditation 91.2, exhorting the Brothers to bear each other's burdens

As I write this note, I am looking west into a smoky sunset, the sun like a orange dye tablet. Trees down the block obscured by smoke, a steady heaving of wind, and then gusts that push all the branches west of a tree's lead, flattening it on one side. The air tastes of smoke. Everywhere I looked, smoke and haze, the neighborhood trees thrashing, then calm; east of our house, Douglas fir and maple surge in another sequence of gusts, more dust, more leaves, twenty feet up, flipping overhead.

This windstorm tonight mirrors an anxiety stirring in me about our city, about our country, and about the coming school year. How can one not be affected?

De La Salle wrote this meditation in three parts for December 30, a time of reflection at year's end. In the second part, De La Salle asks his Brothers to what extent they have borne each other's burdens, shown each other charity, for this is what will hold a community together.

This year of losses, this year of surprises, this year of anguish and worry, this year of promise and rebuilding . . . we go into it together. I cannot imagine it any other way, nor could we hope to sustain ourselves forward without each other.

Sep 6 – 9, 2022
1 message   Mon, Sep 5, 2022 at 8:24 PM

"God in His Providence Has Established the Christian Schools"

St. John Baptist de La Salle
Meditations for The Time of Retreat, title of the first Meditation

On Thursday last week, I walked around the school, snooping. Now that we're back, I was curious . . . what's happening on the third day of school? Well, students were on time to class, teachers noted the day's learning goal; everywhere, everyone stretched their academic muscles.

That same Thursday morning, *The New York Times* published a collection of op-eds called "What Is School For?" where journalists focused on various facets of the American school experience of the last two years. Schools are for everyone, they're about care, upward mobility, learning to read, connecting to nature, based on merit, places of hope; they're about teachers and about parents. My favorite is the last guest opinion, a selfie-pictorial of students from Fremont High School in Oakland called "School Is For Us."

Back in early 18th century France, De La Salle was in his later years, working on the *Meditations for the Time of Retreat,* a guide for the Brothers while they vacationed, a time for spiritual renewal centered on the gifts of the Holy Spirit[9], their gifts, their *charism* carried out every day in the classroom. De La Salle asked that the Brothers not so much look to Jesus' time, but to their own classrooms, their daily work, and their students. He believed deeply in Providence, the mental model of a Catholic school . . . you and your students "entrusted to each other" in your classrooms and offices:

---

[9] 1Cor 12:4-11

"You have been called by God to this ministry, and you have been given the grace of teaching and the gift of exhortation for the sake of those entrusted to your responsibility . . . Use these gifts you have received with care and vigilance."[10]

So . . . what is school for?

What happens in classrooms . . . is made holy by our every faithful exchange with students and each other.

I've always thought what happens in a school is a sacrament in the *Baltimore Catechism* sense of that word, an outward sign of an inward grace. What happens in the classrooms, offices, and hallways of De La Salle appears as a ceaseless current of mundane actions, but is made holy, made sacred by our every faithful exchange with students and each other. We choose it. And being people faithful to our calling, faithful to our unity, we make our school a place where students find themselves, safe, cared for, filled with a sense of belonging, and therefore able to mature in wisdom and grace.

---

[10] *Meditations for the Time of Retreat*, 1.2

Reflecting on September's Lasallian Meme

> "Know your students individually and be able to understand them."
>
> St. John Baptist de La Salle
> *Meditation 33.1*

Think about what it was like for Jean-Baptiste at age 15, a sophomore, on the eve of receiving his canonry, his excitement mixed with anxiety, doubt. Certainly, he was like all teenagers . . . trying to find his way.

Choose a prompt to write about
  ➤ Consider one student you've met in this first month of school who puzzles you, makes you anxious, is a wall of mystery. Write about what you have witnessed from this student, and how you might get to know a little bit more about them.
  ➤ Consider an issue emerging for you this first month; then, *reconsider* it through this Lasallian meme of knowing and understanding your students. What can you or your team do to draw this elusive student into a sense of belonging?

October

an entire fidelity to grace

October

"You can perform miracles in regard to both yourselves and your work – in your own regard, by an entire fidelity to grace, not letting any movement of grace go by without corresponding to it."

St. John Baptist de La Salle – *Meditation 180.3*

By October, the shine is off. Assignments come in, but fewer or hastily done; grades are shallowing out; some students work outside jobs or play on teams where extra commitment strips them of rest; the virtues of punctuality and civility lose their appeal; everywhere, the hinges and latches of school rules and protocols shake loose.

Our second visitation of De La Salle takes place in Paris, early July, 1671. He's 20 and has been away from home less than a year. One evening, he strolls with fellow seminarians on Rue de Sant-Sulpice; the next morning, his dreamed-of-life vanishes with news from Reims.

Where had his graced life gone?

Early on, we imagine our students as young people with bright possibilities. Why wouldn't we? As we "correspond" with them—learn their stories and watch their lives unfold, we see that, at some point, every student stumbles over obstacles teachers cannot see, or are not privy to. We only see the stumble.

These are the graced moments to which our zeal summons us to correspond.

St. Sulpice Seminary
Paris, July 1671

By 1671, a redesigned Èglise Saint Sulpice had been slowly rising for 25 years—tier by tier—a short distance from the Sulpician Seminary where Jean-Baptiste lived. He was 20 years old and far from his family in Reims; he focused entirely on his studies. Evenings, he would walk the Rue Saint-Sulpice with classmates Honoré[11] and Antoine[12], talking about their professors.

It was a relief traveling to Paris and to Saint Sulpice, a respite where his studies of scripture and philosophy now matched the pace and breadth he sought; classes met every day, he was surrounded by the same classmates, at the same hour, on the same topic, and with the same professor. As rhythmic and meditative as the Hours. *I won't be interrupted, won't have to chase a brother, or tell a sister to leave me alone. Just me, under God's most direct watch; each day closer.* In these last weeks of the year's long work – finally – he'd felt the sweet intellectual gallop of a sound argument.

These July evenings between vespers and compline, he and his friends reveled in the walks along the Rue Saint-Sulpice, dusk settling, a breeze off the Seine, arguing about Professor Despériers's[13] thesis, another tangled labyrinth escaping everyone but Antoine.

"I don't get why you don't get it," Antoine said.

Honoré pulled out his snuff box, pinched a smudge to his nostril, and inhaled. *"Merd."* Shook his head and sniffed a second time. "Purposely obscure, I tell you."

Antoine rolled his eyes. "He wants us to work at it, Honoré . . . you shouldn't give up so quickly."

Jean-Baptiste walked between them, watched Honoré brush his nostrils with dusty fingers. "That stuff'll be the death of you."

---

[11] Honoré Azégat was often reprimanded by superiors and left the Sulpicians.

[12] Antoine Brenier was "a child prodigy" and rose high in the Sulpician Society.

[13] Fr. Jacques Despériers was a professor at the Sorbonne and taught De La Salle.

Honoré nodded. "Maybe so," he said, stifling a laugh. "But not for a while . . . and besides . . . Despériers's killing me *right now.*"

Parisians out walking on the Rue Saint-Sulpice that summer's early evening noted three young seminarians coming their way, serious, locked in an animated conversation, who then suddenly tossed their heads in laughter and passed them by.

The heady academics, the morning and evening walks to and from the Sorbonne, the rhythms of the Hours, the warmth of brethren on a communal path—this all evaporated for Jean-Baptiste, once word arrived this morning that, last week, his mother had died.

He slumped in his chair, the news like one of Saint Sulpice's granite blocks thumped into place, a thing that would stand for centuries, holding up a truth that would outlast him, and all his siblings, and the whole of the De La Salle family. He looked at the scaffolding, the pulleys and ropes and dozens of workers scrambling around the stone. It was ceaseless, the work.

Jean-Baptiste queued up another memory, just before he left for Paris, in the family's sitting room as his mother held Jean-Remy, not yet one, his constant crying now blissfully shrouded in sleep.

"Jean-Baptiste," she had said, *"sois un bon prêtre."* Be a good priest.

His eyes ran across his desk, settling first on the day's text, Despériers's *Le Incarnation,* and second on his scrambling notes from class. He pushed back on his desk so that it lurched, and his pen tumbled from its inkwell and dashed a blot of ink on Despériers's text. He watched the page lick it up, bleed to the edge, leech to more pages, then turned his gaze to the unfinished Èglise Saint Sulpice.

Months later, Jean-Baptiste's father dies on April 9, 1672, causing him to leave the seminary. Years later, he returns to his theological studies at the University of Reims and is ordained a priest in April 1678.

Oct 24 – 28, 2011

1 message   Sun, Oct 23, 2011 at 9:14 PM

"[Students] must also be convinced that they themselves are a letter which Jesus Christ dictates to you, which you write each day in their hearts, not with ink, but by the Spirit of the living God, who acts in you through the power of Jesus Christ."

St. John Baptist de La Salle
Meditation for the Time of Retreat, 3.2

I admit that I must read the opening phrase a few times for the metaphor to fully emerge—who is saying what to whom? What is being written? Why does De La Salle emphasize that the students "be convinced" of this?

De La Salle, of course, leans heavily on St. Paul's letter to the wary people of Corinth[14] who were recent converts to a radical religion. Paul described the converts

This is why we are so moved in our work here and sometimes hurt by it.

as the letter contents ("you yourselves are the letter"), the manifest proof of the efficacy of Jesus' story. In his epistle, Paul alludes to Yahweh's Law written on stone tables, but it is Christ's story which supersedes it because Jesus composes directly in one's heart.

This is why we are so moved in our work here and sometimes hurt by it.

Jesus dictates a letter to me . . . and that letter *is my students* . . . and I write that letter not in my heart but *in their hearts.* It is not something that springs from me or is holy about me, but that emanates directly from the "Spirit of the living God." And our students *must be convinced of this.*

---

[14] 2 Cor 3:2-3

Therein is the relationship De La Salle avers about Jesus Christ and student and teacher.

How hard is this?

Well, with some students, our pen runs out of ink, or the tip breaks, or the words vanish as we write them, as if students themselves erase the words. Yet we keep writing. In this mundane world, it is we who must convince students—not always predisposed to hear from adults—that God is active in our relationships with them, that we love them even at their most shrill, unlovable moments. It's why our school is where it is—on the corner of Interstate and Lombard,[15] right where our lives and our students' lives intersect.

---

[15] De La Salle North Catholic High School operated from this North Portland intersection from 2008 to 2021, when it moved to its current location on NE 42nd and Killingsworth.

Oct 7 – 11, 2013

1 message   Sun, Oct 6, 2013 at 9:16 PM

"Remembering that God is with you will help and inspire you in all that you do."

St. John Baptist de La Salle
Letter #2 – to a Brother, 15 May 1701

As we start this sixth week of school—the last of the First Term, there are many moments we might look back upon as illuminations of God's presence in our work. It is likely that our thoughts will be drawn to successes, to moments of breakthrough with a student, for instance. But maybe there are dimmer illuminations—God's presence still—when, in some of our gloomier, darker times, there is only a flicker of light.

Friday morning, a colleague spoke to us about a golden ratio of the teacher-student relationship: 4-to-1. If a student has heard four positive comments from an adult, there's a higher likelihood that student will hear and respond to one correction from that adult. Four positives enable the one correction. This can be very difficult with some students, whose burdens can be so great they cannot carry them alone; these burdens clang and shudder through a school day. So, my 50 colleagues, let's all take up this 4-to-1 challenge, remembering God's presence among us and within each child.

It is sometimes difficult to see our way in this work, to know if we impact a student or can support a colleague. The light we work by can be quite dim. How will we see our way?

"Remember that we are in the Holy Presence of God" . . . and then we can see.

31

Oct 28 – Nov 1, 2013
1 message   Sun, Oct 27, 2013 at 8:51 PM

"Do not have any anxiety about the future. Leave everything in God's hands for He will take care of you."

St. John Baptist de La Salle
Letter #10 – to a young Brother

In De La Salle's time, there was much to worry over; the young religious order was stretched thin to serve increasing requests. A few schools were vandalized, Brother left, some communities had little to eat. Nonetheless, schools thrived. Not without change or severe challenges, of course. The Brothers even survived official dissolution by the French government in the 18th century. The Brothers schools have flourished for over three centuries, from 1680 to this present day in 2013.

Change and loss are endemic to our lot. De La Salle was quite fond of the Sermon on the Mount, especially the section on "the birds of the air' (MT 6: 26-34), and it was often an element of his letters. Perhaps this is why De La Salle himself spoke often of a spirit of faith: "throw yourself into God's arms" (from a Palm Sunday letter), or "Leave the result in God's hands." This Spirit of Faith, that all things we face and especially those times that confound us, must be accepted; we submit ourselves to life's vagaries and yet engage vigorously (even heroically) in teaching the young, faithful that God's love for us, ever present in our beloved community, will sustain us. This is why De La Salle called the Brothers' community "a precious gem."

Let us remember that we are always in the Holy Presence of God . . . as we enter our ninth week of teaching and loving the children entrusted to us.

Oct 13 – 17, 2014
1 message   Sun, Oct 12, 2014 at 9:24 PM

"Let us pray before starting whatever we need to do."

St. John Baptist de La Salle
Meditation 107 – on the Apostle Mathias

Prayer has a long tradition of formality and ritual within the Catholic Church. It's one of the reasons Catholics may stammer when invoking the Almighty without a missal or a breviary. The framework for prayer—codified, organized, and printed in three-year cycles—may seem a peculiar overlay for high school, for in what way does a monastic tradition redound to an American high school?

At the start of each day, we hear the call to prayer. "Staff and students, let's prepare ourselves for prayer."

There's a pause. And then, "Let us remember . . ."

At that remembering, we are also assaying: what is the state of my limited sphere within De La Salle North Catholic High School? How well does the activity and frenetic exuberance of teenagers slow and shush and supplicate? However that might be answered, it is worth noting that that moment is our lone communal moment each day . . . when everyone, in classrooms, in offices, in the hallway, stops and recalls why we do this nearly impossible work. For two minutes each morning, we push away the kinetic, frabjous modern city and call into our hearts the ethereal thrum of monastic prayer. And then we start our beautiful work.

Prayer tethers us to a purpose and that purpose aligns us to a task: touch the hearts and form the minds of those children entrusted to our care.

Oct 3 – 7, 2016

1 message   Sun, Oct 2, 2016 at 8:09 PM

"You can perform miracles in regard to both yourselves and your work—in your own regard, by an entire fidelity to grace, not letting any movement of grace go by without corresponding[16] to it."

St. John Baptist de La Salle
Meditation 180.3 – on the Feast of St. Hilarion

There is so much work to do. All the time, there is work. One looks out to June's horizon . . . and there seems an undulating, limitless sea of planning and papers and decisions. But, deep down, we love it . . . for these are the recurring exchanges we make with the students in our care, our social contract with them, our way of building a sacred trust.

Amid the teeming trivia of paper and assignments that flutter around us, there is a throughput of grace. . . that outward sign of the divine suffused in our communal work with our students. This is what De La Salle refers to in his meditation on the life of St. Hilarion, a 6th century monk who lived in Palestine. What's this really look like, though, this grace? These are just the kids who are here, and I am just the person at De La Salle North Catholic who is here with them. Isn't this just school? Where's the grace in that?

This idea of a continuous, grace-filled relationship with the students in our care—the older brother and sister, as De La Salle often put it—this divine purpose is *central to the idea of Catholic education*. My every exchange with a student is a holy moment, imbued with grace . . . if my heart and

---

[16] When De La Salle uses *correspond*, he refers to the thoughtful correspondence occurring between two people writing letters to each other, an exchange taking place over several weeks. In this way, he references the student-teacher relationship. See the Lasallian meme on page 24.

34

spirit are tuned to a "fidelity to grace." If the ordinary is only and always ordinary, then all this planning and paper is just one empty transaction after another. But we know it's more than that . . . we believe it to be one grace-filled moment after another. This is how miracles occur at De La Salle . . . because you are tuned to everyday grace.

Our students look to you to be reminded of their inner grace.

In this week ahead . . . let's live out this call of our Founder, let's not allow a single "movement of grace go by *without* corresponding to it." Imagine what that will be for our students.

Oct 10 – 14, 2017

1 message
Sun, Oct 9, 2016 at 8:03 PM

"It seems that more and more we shall be exercising our apostolate in a milieu that is de facto pluralistic."

The Declaration: The Brothers of the Christian Schools in the World Today, 1967

Nearly 50 years ago, just after Vatican II, religious orders around the world were rethinking how they should do their work at the dawn of modernity—worldwide, televised communication was instantaneous and widely available. Humanity's population had nearly doubled in the previous 50 years. The millennia-deep, human experience of an insulated life was coming apart. Life ahead would be different.

Viewed from the 21th century, such a notion seems almost quaint. At the heart of *The Declaration's* lament is that modern students "begin with the concrete facts of their own experience" rather than "an abstract ideology, imposed by an external authority." *What the elders tell us is less important than what I experience.* It's worth calling to mind that *The Declaration* spoke about children in the latter half of the 20th century; in other words, they were talking about us. So we ought to know something about this.

Now, we are the ones conducting the work inside the Catholic school, working with students who grew up in a media-saturated environment, and some of that media (Instagram, TikTok, YouTube, et al) is their own creation. It's changing how they think and experience the world.

Our ministry of engaging the spiritual life is our core labor every day.

What, then, is the moral and spiritual ministry we are to conduct? It is a humbling thing to realize that we are but a wee voice in their lives. Unless . . . the relationships we have with our students are strong, and our students believe that being

36

at De La Salle North Catholic is like being part of a family. In this way, our ministry of engaging the spiritual life is our core labor every day.

As our Founder told his young Brothers, "touch hearts" and the miracles follow.

"Look upon those whom God has entrusted to you as God's own children."

St. John Baptist de La Salle
Meditation 133 – on St. Margaret

It's a Lasallian sensibility that goes back to the earliest days . . . our students are the presence of God in our school. So you might wonder, what does that mean, *the presence of God?* After all, there are times when, as even De La Salle occasionally noted, students can be "very far from salvation." We remember that our calling is to see our students through the "eyes of faith," and our faith in them must be unflagging even if the evidence appears to thin out.

Throughout his writings, De La Salle variously notes how the teacher and the student bring God to the other. On the one hand, God has called us to "be ministers and ambassadors of Jesus Christ," to represent Jesus Christ to our students. And on the other hand, the students in our care are "God's own children." Therefore, this most foundational relationship at De La Salle North Catholic is a sign of our Lasallian spirituality.

In another section of this meditation, De La Salle challenged his Brothers about their students: "Do you love them? Do you honor Jesus Christ in their persons?"

Okay, that's sweet and all, but it means what?

It means that once we accept that each student is God present among us, then we act quite differently . . . our Lasallian spirituality forms how we think about our students, how we respond to our students, and how we talk about our students with our peers.

So, our Lasallian spiritual practice this week is to see in each student the presence of God which they may not see in themselves; in this way, when a student looks at you, what she sees is your belief in her reflected back to her.

Oct 9 – 13, 2023
1 message   Sun, Oct 8, 2023 at 9:11 PM

"You can perform miracles in regard to both yourselves and your work—in your own regard, by an entire fidelity to grace, not letting any movement of grace go by without corresponding to it."

St. John Baptist de La Salle
Meditation 180.3 – The Feast of St. Hilarion

It's starting to get real now.

This, the start of week seven and the last of Term 1. Go back in your mind's sense memories—what you heard, what you saw—and there was a shift underway a couple weeks ago. The sheen was off, wasn't it? More evidence was coming in about academic needs in math, reading, writing, as well as a knowledgebase in history. Counseling requests typically ramp up during this time.

We're not alone. Across the US, students struggle mightily (if not historically) in basic skills; we have discovered that holding students to college-ready standards is hard work. Not that this helps in any way, except that what's before us is not solely a De La Salle North Catholic challenge, it's an *everywhere* challenge.

To be true, it's always been this way . . . this reality check at the close of Term 1 (though the amplitude of *this* shift is bigger). Always the strong, sometimes electric start of back-to-school: new students, new seniors, the gang back together doing our Lasallian thing, our deeply sourced communal superpower, and we're feeling it. But what follows closely are the fall-to-earth moments that soon arrive . . . "oh-yeah . . . we have some work to do here."

40

Take heart.

For us, our faithful embrace of the Lasallian heritage starts with a "fidelity to grace," our Spirit of Community being the outward sign of that fidelity. In the Catholic Church, we call this a sacrament, a holy thing, "the outward and visible sign of an inward and invisible grace." It's the through-story of Catholic education—it's holy work, and we should say it out loud. De La Salle taps on this core notion by pointing at *who-we-are-together*: instructional teams conferring with each other, two teachers talking about how to teach close reading, Level Teams strategizing consistent messaging, teachers and counselors meeting with parents and students . . . outward signs of the spirit of community we embrace.

If September was about discovering our students, then October—feeling the weight of our challenges—is about our fidelity to grace . . . that we ought not allow "a movement of grace to go by without corresponding to it."[17]

God bless you and our Lasallian community in its grace-filled, beautiful work.

---

[17] The Lasallian meme (p. 24) describes how teachers ought to "correspond" with what he called a "movement of grace," a moment that calls a teacher to intervene on behalf of students in need.

"Time starts now."

The Words That Start Each SAT Exam

During the SAT test last Wednesday in the gymnasium, I looked out at our 51 seniors taking their seats, each one three feet distant from others. They yawned and looked around, stretched their necks and legs, rolled their shoulders. A few late comers wandered amid the table scheme looking for their name, classmates head-nodding directions.

I wondered, will it show itself here? And so I started to think about what I look for, when I'm looking for De La Salle North Catholic.

- What are the signals of a Lasallian Catholic community?
- What are the artifacts of our charism of faith and zeal, that spiritual gift that is distinctly Lasallian?

I look for how we care for each other, what De La Salle repeatedly called upon the Brothers to do . . . something we can only do by a conscious choice driven by our faith in God, in each other, and in our students – especially in the hardest moments of what we do.

I look for how we care for our students, that most obvious spiritual act you have conducted a thousand, thousand times each day when you look our students in the eye, speak their name, hear and hold their story, and affirm their dignity—especially when that's hard to do.

Wednesday morning, I witnessed their earnestness with the task, their friendship and encouragement of each other, their simpatico with the test monitors and, really, with all of you.

So, let me ask you, what do you look for, when you go looking for De La Salle North Catholic?

Reflecting on October's Lasallian Meme

> "You can perform miracles in regard to both yourselves and your work – in your own regard, by an entire fidelity to grace, not letting any movement of grace go by without corresponding to it."
>
> St. John Baptist de La Salle – *Meditation 180.3*

Think about the day before De La Salle hears of his mother's death. He was in the thrall of a bright intellectual life. In an instant, life's unrelenting reality hits like a stone—his mother is dead. The very idea of study, once a pleasure, is suddenly repellant.

Choose a prompt to write about

> Consider one student whose hard story you have recently learned or whose persona is sharply amiss. Write about what you have witnessed from this student, and how you or your team might be able to help.

> Write about a theme emerging for you this second month; then, consider it through this Lasallian meme of a moment of grace to which and your team might correspond.

November

do not be disheartened

November

"You must take care not to be disheartened by difficulties.
On the contrary, you ought to humble yourself in view of your weakness and turn to God, in whom and by whom you can do everything.
Firm courage and a little generosity will enable you to
overcome your difficulties."

St. John Baptist de La Salle – *Letter #90, to a Brother*

School is hard. Over time, difficulties mount. Our students are among hundreds of peers from a wide continuum of family experience, each one its own dynamic of family and friends, of loving care and dire neglect, if not occasional abuse. Add social media as students' primary filter of their world, the students in our care walk up the school's steps a tangled mass of woe and worry. It's morning, and here they come again.

Do I have what it takes to teach today?

In this third visitation, we meet the newly ordained Father De La Salle. In the first weekend of April 1678, a few weeks shy of turning 27, he fulfills his life's dream to be a priest followed two weeks later by grief's return. What now?

In our time, difficulties shadow our work among students. What now?

This Lasallian meme speaks to your "firm courage and generosity" that sustains us in the shadows of our calling.

⊕   ⊕   ⊕

Motherhouse, Sisters of the Child Jesus
Reims, April 23, 1678

It is mid-morning on Saturday, 23 April 1678. Two weeks prior, the 26-year-old Jean-Baptiste de La Salle had been ordained, his winding-path dream finally realized. His siblings and extended family were there, as were his friends, among them Fr. Nicolas Roland, fellow Cathedral canon and De La Salle's spiritual advisor. Since that festive day, rumors percolated through the Reims citizenry about scarlet fever in the Champagne region. Then, in recent days, it was so . . . the dread illness had reached the Motherhouse of the Sisters of the Child Jesus, a few blocks from the Cathedral.

Père De La Salle watched as a shaft of sunlight fell in the apse, thinned, disappeared, and then reappeared across from him. It had been a cold rain for days and this sunlight seemed a sign that God had remembered this new priest. As his eyes followed the dust motes swim up through the incense, his mind wandered to his friend Nicolas Roland. Earlier, on his way to sing terce, a sister from the Motherhouse called to him at the canon's portal.

"Pardon, Mon Père de La Salle, un instant."

Startled, De La Salle turned to her as she continued. "Fr. Roland has called for you," she said. She held his eyes a moment, mute, then spoke again. *"Rapidement."* And then was gone.

In his choir seat, De La Salle tapped the stall's armrest and then rose with his fellow canons. Their plaintive chant rang in the cathedral nave.

I have lifted up my eyes to the mountains
From whence shall help come to me.[18]

Afterward, De La Salle walked below the cathedral's rose window and turned south on his way to the Motherhouse on the Rue de Barbàtre to see his friend. De La Salle had heard that a fever had swept among the

---

[18] Psalm 121

sisters and students. *It has struck Nicolas, I am sure . . . why else the haste?* Though deep amid these harried thoughts, he kept his measured, public pace. Blue sky broke through scattering clouds. Drips from trees and shrubs pattered like an occasional shower. Birdsong. Sunlight cast some warmth on his shoulder as he sloshed along the road, mud sputtering up on his boots and cassock, as the psalmist's words played in his head.

My help is from the Lord . . .

He remembered Nicolas' help after his father's death six years past. Having left St. Sulpice, De La Salle returned home as the family's elder, the seminary behind him. In time, his friend's counsel opened a path to his ordination, celebrated two weeks ago in the Archbishop's palace chapel. Nicolas was there, clasping his hands, ready to receive his blessing.

"God bless you, my brother," he had said.

Along the road, lavender heads and hawthorn buds were in flower, pale green shoots of early spring pulsed everywhere. De La Salle passed the Collège of his early years, those times from a decade ago, as a boy running these streets in the early morning on his way to class. He shook off the memory. With each step closer to the Motherhouse, the sweeping pride and exhilaration of his ordination faded. He felt his Roman collar stiff against the wart on his neck, a satisfying annoyance. At the Motherhouse door, he knocked.

Sister Anne greeted him. *"Bienvenu, Mon Père de La Salle."*

She led him through a hallway where fever smells assailed him, past the chapel and into the small cell where Nicolas lay. A side table held a bowl of water, a kettle, and a cup filled with chamomile tea. Sister Françoise, the Superior, attended him while the young Nicolas Rogier[19] sat in a chair against the wall.

"My brother . . . De La Salle."

"Mon Frère Roland, such sadness to see you so ill."

---

[19] Fellow canon Nicolas Rogier was to be the second executor of Roland's will.

De La Salle pulled a chair next to the bed and sat. He saw the distress in his friend's eyes. A thin sweat and red rash sheathed this face; every few breaths, he'd wince and click his tongue.

De La Salle tapped his own throat with his forefinger, whispered, "Your throat?"

Nicolas nodded.

Sister Françoise handed De La Salle a wet cloth. He turned to her. *"Merci."* And added. "How many days?"

"Quatre."

At that, De La Salle tilted his head, pursed his lips. Roland struggled to clear his throat and propped one elbow to lift himself. Coughed again and settled back to his pillow. He lay quiet for a moment.

"Mon Frère De La Salle, Canon Rogier . . . *kuh-kuh* . . . I request . . . that you be the executors of my will . . . "

Rogier opened his mouth, appearing to object, but De La Salle quickly raised his hand to him, *non.* Roland shifted his shoulders, then motioned to Sister Françoise who handed an envelope to De La Salle.

Roland nodded. "It's all there." His eyes opened wide, a wince. "My back," he said, then continued. "Most important, mon frère . . . you are to take on chaplaincy for the Sisters."

He took another breath, and De La Salle daubed his forehead.

"There's money for the Congregation." A breath. "To be recognized in the Chur- . . . *kuh-kuh* . . . funded." He swallowed. "And keep the girls' school[20] open."

De La Salle nodded. Nicolas raised his left arm and reached across his chest to hold his friend's arm. "See to it."

"Oui."

For a few minutes they talked of next things – details in his will, the finances for the sisters' community and the school. Already, De La Salle saw the tasks ahead, starting with an audience with Archbishop Le Tellier.

---

[20] The Sisters of the Child Jesus ran a free school for girls on their property.

Roland's eyelids drooped, sleep just on the other side there. A few full, slow breaths. He opened his eyes. His tongue, white at the tip and edges, slipped across his lower lip. De La Salle looked at his friend and then lifted the cup of tea to his mouth.

In the 11 months following Nicolas Roland's death, De La Salle fulfilled his executorship by confirming the donors for the Sisters of the Child Jesus, purchasing a building for them, and renewing several of their leases; in addition, he negotiated with city councilors and Archbishop Le Tellier for the establishment of their community which was ratified by all parties in August. In February 1679, King Louis XIV signed the *lettres patent,* thus granting official legitimacy to the Order. As Roland requested, De La Salle took up the chaplaincy for the Sisters.

Nov 22 – 24, 2010
1 message   Sun, Nov 21, 2010 at 8:57 PM

"The way to find the real "world" is . . . to find your own inner ground."

Thomas Merton
Contemplation in a World of Action, 1971

When a student leaves our school, regardless of the reason, we all suffer the loss. Of course, we have done all we can do—our compassion guides us to help as deeply and thoroughly as a group of adults can. But our students' lives away from De La Salle North Catholic can be so broken that all our efforts are sometimes insufficient to bind a wound or forestall an action. Just in the last two weeks, five students left our school. I do not believe we could have done any more to keep a single one.

Each story differs, each circumstance a reminder to me of De La Salle's famous acknowledgment in *The Conduct of The Christian Schools*: "our students' lives are sometimes too burdensome for them to bear." Still, I am confident that our community has touched them, helped them in some way.

What a paradox November is . . . a time of re-   *Faith helps us*
membrance and thanksgiving. We face our   *stand there.*
losses, and we give thanks for life. Faith helps us
stand there. This seems clearly what Thomas Merton sought in his contemplative life: an "inner ground" on which he stood, a place of faith amid a clamoring and confounding world.

⊕   ⊕   ⊕

Nov 12 – 15, 2013

1 message   Sun, Nov 11, 2013 at 8:42 PM

"The young should be able to see in your wisdom how they should behave."

St. John Baptist de La Salle
Meditation 132.1 – on the feast of St. Norbert

It was not until De La Salle realized his little start-up schools were in trouble due to untrained young Brothers that he focused much of his life thereafter on what we now call "professional development." Someone at our principals gathering at Mont La Salle mentioned this idea, and I was lost for a few minutes in the idea of 18th century Professional Development. I'd been so disposed to think of professional development as a 20th century phenomenon—and a *late* 20th century development—that this notion seemed at first strange to contemplate.

However, one need only look upon De La Salle's writing to understand that professional development was at the core of his work: *The Conduct of the Christian Schools* was a best seller for nearly two centuries and was entirely about how to run a school well; his *Meditations for Time of Retreat* are designed for a 16-day summer retreat that challenged Brothers to examine their instruction. His letters are replete with instructional suggestions for young Brothers, with remonstrations of thinned-skinned school leaders, and directives for older Brothers who'd later become School Inspectors.

He understood intuitively that a well-run classroom existed within a well-tuned school culture . . . and that took training and patience to achieve.

⊕   ⊕   ⊕

Nov 24 – 26, 2014

1 message   Sun, Nov 23, 2014 at 7:03 PM

"You must take care not to be discouraged by your difficulties, my very dear Brother. On the contrary, you ought to humble yourself in view of your weakness and turn to God, in whom and by whom you can do everything."

St. John Baptist de La Salle
Letter #90 – to an unnamed Brother

We are two-thirds through Semester One, Monday being the first day of the 3rd Term. Maybe you can sit back, close your eyes, and recline your head on the sweet air of early September, a time when all was aglow with the possible. Today, we look straight into what's real, man. Hopeful, but tempered, yes, with the scars and limitations of what has passed and what we know. In such a time, De La Salle's words come as both balm and reminder. I can scarcely imagine the welter of woe that daily fell upon the Brothers in rural 18th century France.

At the last Student Review[21] meeting, the team reviewed 51 students, the largest group being seniors. Many of those seniors our community has been assisting for over three years . . . and we'll probably keep them in our arms right through to graduation. It's the kind of thing that may pitch one into despondency. But none of our work has a linear response to collective effort. Sometimes, there is so much of a deficit to overcome or the systemic resistance so great—familial, academic, social, or psychological—that all our collective effort may only result in not falling further or not falling as fast. What can one do, but the very best we can and then "turn to God, in whom and by whom [we] can do everything."

---

[21] The Student Review is a weekly meeting of administrators, counselors, and Work Study leaders who discuss supports for the school's most vulnerable students.

Nov 2 – 6, 2015

1 message   Sun, Nov 1, 2015 at 8:36 PM

"Let it be clear, then, in all your relations with the children who are entrusted to you that you look upon yourself as ministers of God, acting with love, with a sincere and true zeal, accepting with much patience the difficulties you have to suffer, willing to be dishonored and mistreated, even to give your life for Jesus in the fulfillment of your ministry."

St. John Baptist de La Salle
Meditations for the Time of Retreat, 9.1

Every person who has a connection to De La Salle North Catholic High School makes a sacrifice of some kind: teachers, counselors, cooks, students, drivers, maintenance, parents, donors, coaches. Everyone offers some part of their personal time and spirit in this sacred work to change a life. The closer any one of us is to the child, the more difficult the work, the more resistance there sometimes is and, consequently, the more doubt that naturally will seep into the thin cracks of our spirit and zeal.

When we accept a child, we accept a promise to serve. When a family decides to come to De La Salle North Catholic, there comes with that decision an expectation of change. It may be that the child does not yet see it, cannot comprehend what change is needed, the self so misunderstood or misidentified that no trust is ever extended. But around this child, there are *many who do see it*, who do comprehend the needed change, and who do trust us to help. And so, when we accept a child, we accept a promise to serve.

Installing a drinking fountain with fill station; returning a phone call to a parent; helping a student—for the ninth time—learn how to compute negative exponents; making sure auditors have what they need as a way to ensure our financial practices are sound; being on time to a meeting or a prefecting spot; or making double-sure that an email to a parent is accurate and has no grammatical errors. We complete these tasks because we believe in our Lasallian mission, and our daily work is an expression of how we serve.

All of it matters . . . because all of it sends a message of belief, of our inherent belief in the deep value of every child in our care, especially for those we think may not want to be here or don't yet know *how* to be here.

Can we not, right now, list a handful of students who seem beyond what we can muster? It is to these students most of all that our best selves must go. St. La Salle reminds us to "accept with much patience the difficulties [we'll] have to suffer."

This week, with love and zeal, lean into the toughest work you will face.

Nov 16 – 20, 2015

1 message   Sun, Nov 15, 2015 at 10:11 PM

"To touch the hearts of your pupils and to inspire them with the Christian spirit is the greatest miracle you can perform, and one which God expects of you."

St. John Baptist de La Salle
Meditation 139.3 – on the Feast of St. Peter

A Christian spirit . . . it is worth remembering that the Christian call is to live as Jesus lived and taught, not as, say, contemporary prelates do.

When De La Salle exhorted his young Brothers to "touch the hearts of your pupils," he plucked the chord of an educational truth—the example of morally mature adults is what deeply teaches. By way of example, is it not true that our students are keenly (if not obsessively) attuned to "what is fair" . . . that how we establish, monitor and mitigate what is fair in classrooms, hallways, offices, athletic fields and courts is on display, every day, all the time. It is this "implicit curriculum" by which our students most consistently know and trust us. This we could not do were it not for a shared moral vision.

Yes, De La Salle North Catholic High School does publish and teach a full academic program. If that were all, however, then let's fold up our sign, close the school, and join ranks with Portland Public Schools. But no . . . we have a calling to grace—to live out loud, and in community, as a school whose elemental work emerges from a moral and theological mission. It is *who-we-are-together* that is the miracle for our students.

We engender such a sacramental life because our very presence is both repository and dispensary of God's presence in their frenetic, heavy lives.

This we can do only when we con-
sciously embrace that moral and theological history as a community . . . and
why this Thursday coming up is so critical for our school. Our second Great
Conversation[22] will be the second
Lasallian Core Principle, "Concern for
the Poor and Social Justice." In so do-

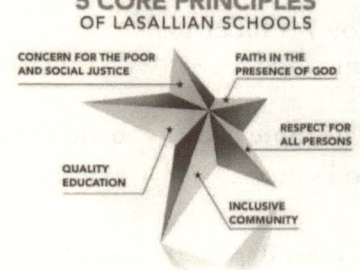

ing, we call to mind the many ways we are in solidarity with the poor and
advocate for those suffering from injustices. Such a coming together cultivates our shared moral vision. This is the miracle God expects of us.

Many years ago, at a time of entrenched personal uncertainty, a mentor
counseled me: practice gratefulness each day, and the way will come clear.
We come each day to this corner of North Lombard and Interstate never
knowing what may come, but we have made a moral commitment to our
students. In this November, therefore, let's practice being grateful. Pick
one or two or more students . . . be grateful for their presence in your
life.

In this way, we offer thanksgiving to the students and families who call
out the goodness us.

---

[22] A year-long series of whole staff study and discussion on each of the Five Core
Principles of Lasallian Schools. Image is from the DLSI website.

Nov 7 – 10, 2016
1 message   Sun, Nov 6, 2016 at 6:06 PM

"The more loving you are to the young, the greater will be the effects of God's grace."

St. John Baptist de La Salle
Meditation 134.2 – on St. Barnabas

Friday morning from the back stoop, there were about three minutes of spectacular morning color daubed on the eastern horizon, dazzling strata I could see through trees and buildings, as the sun broke over the Cascades. It was that far off gaze that helped me notice a handful of our students get off their bus at Lombard and Interstate. None waited for any others . . . it was five separate students getting off their morning ride on the way to school.

As they strode down Lombard's sidewalk, their distances from each other lengthened, so that they stretched out to just over three fence posts from first walker to last. A couple of them wore headphones. All of them faced forward, not looking left or right; not pausing or speeding up, never uttering a word to anyone else . . . an equidistant morning solitude held them together. I wondered what they were carrying this Friday morning; maybe, they were just tired and wanted their space. Even so, I wondered . . . what from home came with them . . . what lay ahead for them at school . . . what larger, gnawing, unknowable narrative made that solitary walk to school what it was?

De La Salle wrote in his *The Conduct of the Christian Schools,* a line I've quoted before: "It often happens that students do not have enough strength of body or of mind to bear the burdens which many times overwhelm them." It is worth noting that this line appears in his "Introductory Remarks on Corrections," where he advises Brothers about balancing gentleness and firmness. As Lasallians, we know that both approaches are effective only to the extent we are in a trusted relationship with our students. Only in that trust might we ever hear about that unknowable narrative and might we be able to help them carry it.

Nov 28 – Dec 2, 2016
1 message   Sun, Nov 27, 2016 at 8:39 PM

"For our salvation is nearer now than when we first believed. The night is advanced, the day is at hand. Let us throw off the works of darkness and put on the armor of light."

Romans 13:12

We have passed into a new year.

Within the Catholic Church, the First Sunday of Advent opens the Liturgical Year, when the Church begins the yearlong narrative of our salvific history within the natural catalog of Earth's seasonal changes. In these last weeks of fall, just as darkness spreads to its fullest grip of our day, we light a weekly candle, four before Christmas, a reminder that Light is coming, a New Day will soon dawn.

Weekly, night holds on longer while day slips to night more quickly. And so we light more candles, a symbolic action against the dark, a metaphor of the quickening Light we bring to our students and families.

The holiday season is a time of heightened anxiety for many of our students. In the three weeks before Christmas Break, students' worries and stressors abound. The holiday season is a time of heightened anxiety for many of our students. Last Wednesday was the last day of Term Two, the twelfth week of the school year. Perhaps you've already seen some signs: falling grades, worries about extended time in a chaotic home, sullenness, outbursts, ennui, quitting or threatening to quit, talk of transferring. These are young people whose vision has adjusted to a deepening dark.

Light your candle. Light two. And put them both on a pedestal.

60

We are part of a very long narrative . . . the opening stanzas of a young person's epic life story. After a grim and damp November, how redemptive might our work be, to our students and to us, if what we do is suffuse our community with Light and Hope?

Nov 13 – 17, 2017
1 message   Sun, Nov 12, 2017 at 9:13 PM

"Thank God for the grace he has given you in your work."

St. John Baptist de La Salle
Meditations for the Time of Retreat, 7.3

There are times when what you do receives no notice.

You work on lessons, read dozens of papers, speak to 20 prospective Corporate Work Study employers, compile financial reports, prepare notes and reports for Board Members, repair sinks and toilets and doors only to see them broken again, listen to parents worry about their child or question what you do or what you decided. In a school, as in life, not everything is blue skies and butterflies.

In a school, it's never about one day or a couple of days, but about all of the days. What you and your trusted, hardworking *Working in a school means taking a long view.*
colleagues do through the travails of a *whole* academic year is what touches lives, what connects you and them and all of us to the students in our care. Working in a school means taking a long view. It's a lot like family. Not all days are good, but—if carried out with grace—*all of them together* are.

Come Monday, there are ten days until Thanksgiving. I would like you to join me in ten days of saying "Thank You" to our colleagues and to our students, without whom God's grace goes wanting. These are our days of gratitude . . . a word, a note, a cheery cup of coffee . . . thank you for working alongside me . . . thank you for being a student in my class . . . thank you for sending your children to our school . . . thank you for hiring our students . . . thank you for your financial support . . . thank you for helping me figure something out . . . thank you for listening to me. A thousand thank-yous.

Thank you, dear colleagues, for your grace in this beautiful work. I am so glad you are all here.

⊕　⊕　⊕

Nov 5 – 9, 2018
1 message   Sun, Nov 4, 2018 at 8:41 PM

"You have been called by God to this ministry and you have been given the grace of teaching and the gift of exhortation for the sake of those entrusted to your responsibility."

St. John Baptist de La Salle
Meditations for the Time of Retreat, 1.2

Being "called by God" is maybe not all it's cracked up to be. The Old and New Testaments are strewn with the names of people whose lives were turned upside down or flat out destroyed because God tapped them on the shoulder: "You there, come 'ere, I need you to do something for Me."

Pardon the tongue-in-check, but let's face it . . . God's calls are not for the faint of heart. The ask will be big. Just look around . . . consider what you do in a typical week or two.

This is why the second half of De La Salle's statement resonates: "You have been given the grace of teaching and the gift of exhortation."

The problem is that graces and gifts are not always readily known by the recipient, may in fact be not developed at all. This, too, is true of the people God chooses . . . we tend not to believe we have what God says we have.

This meme—*the chosen do not feel ready*—meets its match in Lasallian education when De La Salle, early in his work, realizes that a well-formed group of educators—*as a community*—can in fact do the work to which they have been called. This is why the "you" in De La Salle's writing is best understood as the second-person plural . . . he is talking about all of us together, union in our one community, our precious gem.

Let's teach and exhort. Let's call them by name, let's name their sacred and dignified selves . . . and let their dignified selves build up the future we hope for.

Nov 16 – 20, 2020
1 message   Sun, Nov 15, 2020 at 8:32 PM

"You must not only pray for yourself but also for those whom you are guiding."

St. John Baptist de La Salle
Meditation 187.2 – on the Feast of St. Charles Borromeo

At the start of our Admin Team meeting on Tuesday and the Student Review Team meeting on Thursday, we took turns and spoke aloud the name of a student we carry in our hearts.

"J_____."

"B_____."

We know each one, and we know a part of their story. In that quiet time after "Let us remember . . . that we are in the Holy Presence of God," our heart wanders through the interactions and anxiety we carry for the many students out near the guardrails, not sure if or how they can pull themselves away from the precipice.

"M___."

"L___."

It is the DNA of this amazing school and your own spiritual makeup that calls you to De La Salle North Catholic . . . so that every day brings us in providential contact with young people holding on. There have always been, and there always will be, students entangled in our school's support apparatus, fumbling, avoiding . . . or students who, as De La Salle wrote in his *Conduct of the Christian Schools*, "do not have enough strength of body or mind to bear the burdens which many times over-whelm them."[23] How much more so now?

"W_____."

"C_____."

A little over two weeks ago at Family Conferences, teachers, counselors, and administrators met with 43 students and their families . . . over the next few weeks, we meet up with many of those students and families again to check in: how are you doing? Are you caught up with read-ing/homework/quizzes? Sometimes the news is good; sometimes it's not. Here, at the semester's mid-point and vexed by online learning, we sense our limits.

"D_____."

"T_____"

And so we stay at the tasks, and pray for our students, and pray for our colleagues, each of you who work so ingeniously hard to support our students. De La Salle was right to call his Brothers to prayer, especially as challenges grew, especially as crises (famine, loss of a school, et al) opened at their feet, causing students to stumble away from them. On-ward we go, in faith and zeal.

In this month of remembrance and gratitude, who are the names on your weekly sticky note?

⊕   ⊕   ⊕

---

[23] De La Salle, John Baptist. *The Conduct of the Christian Schools*, p 136.

Reflecting on November's Lasallian Meme

> "You must take care not to be disheartened by difficulties. On the contrary, you ought to humble yourself in view of your weakness and turn to God, in whom and by whom you can do everything. Firm courage and a little generosity will enable you to overcome your difficulties."
>
> St. John Baptist de La Salle – *Letter #90, to a Brother*

De La Salle had been a priest barely two weeks when word came that his friend and mentor Fr. Nicolas Roland lay dying in the convent where he was chaplain. Roland surprised De La Salle by requesting that he be the executor of his will, which meant taking over his chaplaincy and providing for the continuance of the school run by the sisters.

Choose a prompt to write about.

➤ Write about a time when your workload shifted, you felt put-upon or not equal to the new task; or, a set of new difficulties vex your work, seem to undo or neutralize your best efforts. Describe what you or your team might do—with "firm courage and a little generosity"—to support you and/or your students.

➤ Consider an issue emerging for you in this third month; then, write about it through this Lasallian lens of taking care of yourself amid difficulties, returning to your spiritual center to take heart and reset.

December

knocking at the door

December

"How long has Jesus been knocking at the door of your heart,
waiting to enter?"

St. John Baptist de La Salle
Meditation 85.1 – For the Vigil of the Nativity of Jesus Christ

Even as a mythos, there's a grip there—how the students' presence in our lives is a continuous knocking, such that the more persistent, urgent, even desperate knocking seems a call we must answer one way or another . . . yes, no. One might be tempted to ignore it; but that is, of course, itself an answer. The always knocking. In our classroom. In our office. In the hallway, the Front Office, or sitting on the stoop at 5:00 PM waiting for a pickup.

In this fourth visitation, De La Salle, now 27 and a priest for eleven months, arrives at the door of the Motherhouse of the Sisters of the Child Jesus about the same time as Adrien Nyel, a visitor from out of town. From this threshold moment forward, everything changes for De La Salle. His life is headed, incrementally, on a different arc. He has no idea what's coming.

To what extent are you prepared to open your classroom door?

This Lasallian meme is a call to listen carefully, be aware of the subtle signs of need which have crept into our students' lives and overwhelmed them such that they do not know what to do.

The Motherhouse of the Sisters of the Child Jesus
Reims, March 1679

The previous year had been full of meetings and leases and negotiations getting the Sisters of the Child Jesus established as an official religious enterprise and their school up and running. But it was done.

Father De La Salle turned his attention to being a priest: leading processions, singing in the choir, officiating at High Masses. He had settled in as Cathedral canon, spiritual advisor, and chaplain for the Sisters, which was why, on this morning in early March, he was on his way to the Motherhouse.

Anyone walking the Rue de Barbâtre that morning would have seen an older man at the Motherhouse door, waiting, looking around; and with him, a boy, the man's right hand resting on his shoulder. He knocked at the door, looked down at the boy, knocked again. Shook his hand as if to cast the knock's sting from it, pulled the cuff lace of his brown frock, and looked down the street where he saw a young priest approaching, a measured gait.

The priest was early that morning. He left his choir stall right after mid-morning prayer, relishing his careful walk to the Motherhouse along l'Université, past St. Patrick's Hall and the Notre Dame convent when he noticed, about 30 meters off, two people standing at the Motherhouse door. As he neared, his initial thought faded; the pair were not father and son . . . more likely grandfather and grandson. Distracted by a sudden pungency, he looked down, sidestepped a horse dropping, wagged his head, smiled, then kept walking, his gait back on stride just in time to put his foot on the stoop.

The priest doffed his hat and turned to the stranger. *"Bonjour."*
The stranger nodded. *"Bonjour, mom frère.*

Just then, Sister Anne[24] opened the door. The priest deferred, allowing the two guests to enter ahead of him.

Inside and having some time, the priest walked to the chapel and sat in a pew along the chapel's back wall. The air damp enough to make him sneeze, then cough. He cleared his throat and closed his eyes. Minutes pass, then footsteps. In the corridor, coming his way.

Someone at the door. *"Excusez-moi, Mon Père."*

It was Sister Anne, her eyes directed at the floor. "Sister Françoise has asked that you come to the parlor to meet someone." They walked from the small chapel with its low-slung ceiling, the priest following as he exited behind Sister Anne.

As they entered the parlor, Sister Françoise stepped forward. The priest noted the stranger he'd met at the door, raised his eyebrows to acknowledge him and then addressed the good sister.

"Sister Françoise, so good to see you." The priest gave the slightest bow, holding his hat with both hands.

"Ah, *Mon Père* . . . gracious always . . . *merci.*" She turned to the stranger, now standing. "Monsieur Nyel, let me introduce you," then turned to the young priest, extending her arm, "to Père De La Salle."

Nyel lifted his head, side-eyeing him. *"Bonjour à nouveau, mon frère."* And points to the front door. "Didn't I . . . we . . ."

De La Salle nodded. *"Oui, Monsieur."*

Sister Anne returned to the room with a platter of tea, a small loaf, some cheese and set it on a small table. She paused, looked at the two men, motioning to the tray. *"S'il te plait."*

"Gentlemen," said Sister Françoise. "I believe the two of you have something in common. Sister Anne and I shall leave you to it."

"Ehm . . . well . . . yes," began Nyel, gesturing to an open chair. "Père De La Salle . . . please join me."

As Nyel circled the table to his seat, he stated his business. "I have

---

[24] Sister Anne Lecoeur had accompanied Sister Françoise Duval who came to Reims in 1670 to start an orphanage for poor girls.

heard you're the one to talk to about starting a school in Reims." He continued for a few minutes about a school for boys, how it would serve the families in Reims, and how the Maillefer family was willing to support it. He stopped and reached for tea and bread. He pulled off a piece of bread and started to eat. For a long moment, quiet filled the room.

"I wasn't expecting a proposal like this, Monsieur." De La Salle sipped some tea. *The Council will not want to do this,* he thought. *It is too much, too soon.* He set his cup down, followed Nyel's eyes to the door, then leaned in. "We do need such a school here. However," his left hand up, the forefinger pointed, "I do not believe there's an appetite for this, at least not now.'

He sat back, then continued. "It was only a few weeks ago, after years of Monsieur Roland's efforts, and my insistence after his death that we implored His Excellency the Archbishop to help . . . that the King, weeks ago, signed the Sisters' *lettres patent.*" [25]

He exhaled. Across the table, Nyel sat motionless, taking in the news, dropping his eyes to some crumbled cheese on the table. For a beat or two no one spoke. *So . . . this is the guy Madame Maillefer[26] says can help me. Took me four days to get here . . . now, in ten minutes, I'm told this probably won't work.*

De La Salle felt the impasse. "Where are you staying?"

Nyel looked up. "What?"

"You've come from Rouen, some days travel." He caught his eye and recalled the boy in the corridor. "Young Christopher[27], I'm sure, is exhausted . . . and . . ."

"Madame Maillefer has said I can stay with her brother Monsieur Dubois[28], so . . ."

---

[25] *Lettres Patent,* published document granting an official recognition of legitimacy.

[26] Née Jeanne Dubois in Reims, Madame Maillefer was a wealthy benefactress of gratuitous schools in Rouen and related by marriage to the De La Salle family.

[27] Probably Christopher, a "teacher for Monsieur De La Salle" who was buried on May 15, 1682, in Saint-Symphorien parish. See Bernard Hours, p 122.

[28] Christophe Dubois, brother to Madama Maillefer, related by marriage to Nicolas Roland.

De La Salle had reached for his cup of tea as Nyel dropped the name. *"Non!"*

"What?"

"You cannot do this . . . it will all end if you stay there."

Nyel grimaced. "What do you mean?"

Aware he was brusque, De La Salle settled in his chair. "Ehm . . . I mean . . . it was hard, very hard, to do this last year . . . we needed the Archbishop and the City Council. This time, we need a quieter strategy."

They fell silent again.

"Look . . . I understand," Nyel said. Tapped his forehead a couple of times and sighed. "Perhaps I'll just stay overnight to recoup and then be on my way to Rouen."

"No need." De La Salle motioned with his right hand. "Stay with me . . . at my house a few blocks away. No one will take note of you there. You and your companion . . . you can rest . . . and we can talk more."

"But . . ." Nyel interrupted.

De La Salle waved him off and leaned across the table. "The need is great here, no doubt . . . but the timing, I'm afraid, is not propitious. Still, the need." He trailed off, looked out the window. "Stay at my house . . . there are some people I know . . . maybe there is something we can do."

For several days, De La Salle and Adrien Nyel met with local pastors to discuss starting a school for boys without the City Council's oversight. Their solution was to find a local parish willing to hire and house teachers. After considering many options, they chose an eager Nicolas Dorigny, pastor of Saint-Maurice, and the school opened on April 15. By December, Nyel and De La Salle opened a second school for poor boys in another Reims parish, Saint-Jacques.

Dec 3 – 7, 2012
1 message   Sun, Dec 2, 2012 at 8:55 PM

"God has chosen you to do this work."

St. John Baptist de La Salle
Meditations for the Time of Retreat, 4.2

We've each started differently on the path to De La Salle North Catholic: responded to an ad or listened to a cajoling friend. In themselves, these are mundane events, regular things, differing very little in stature from doing laundry or cleaning the gutters or going shopping. And so it comes across as strange to consider being at De La Salle North Catholic as a calling, *as from God.*

Now that we're in the 13th week of Semester One, the notion that one is *called* to this work may seem even more remote—we and our students are tired, few if any moments sparkle with divine light, and more than a few moments bear a tremor of chaos and futility. One might even question, am I fit to do this work?

Enter Advent, in Latin, *to arrive.* So let these days ahead before our break be those days of spiritual imagination— *Let your very presence be the proof of God's call.* let your very presence be the proof of God's call. Our diet need not consist of locusts and honey, but our humility and courage ought to mirror John's hope.

Have a good and gentle week.

⊕   ⊕   ⊕

Dec 16 – 20, 2013

1 message   Sun, Dec 15, 2013 at 9:26 PM

Friday, December 13, Br. Mark Murphy, FSC, former Visitor of the San Francisco District, led a morning retreat for the staff.

"Do you have such faith that it is able to touch the hearts of your students and to inspire them with the Christian spirit? This is the greatest miracle you could perform, and the one that God asks of you, since this is the purpose of your work."

St. John Baptist de La Salle
Meditation 139.3 – on the Feast of the St. Peter

The light tympani in my ears are the exhortations of Br. Mark who, on the behalf of the Brothers, invited us to follow in faith the incremental nudging of Providence. In "the eyes of Faith," one can see the dimly perceptible trace of God's action to bring us to North Portland, to work in this community with our students and families. Some of our daily challenges present as intractable and occasionally leave us exasperated. Howsoever we might seek help, ultimately, we are the ones here. As Brother Mark reminded us, the Lasallian charism of zeal compels us to act for the young people who are "far from salvation."

At the core of the Lasallian charism are the relationships we form with our students. No single student should ever walk among us without a committed adult who knows well the life he or she leads. It is this "sense of belonging" that students cherish, why they speak of De La Salle North Catholic as family. Knowing a student well helps us when we must correct that student—shall we be gentle, shall we be firm, or shall we find a means to be both?

Dec 8 – 12, 2014

1 message   Sun, Dec 7, 2014 at 7:34 PM

"You must pray not only for yourself but for those you are guiding."

St. John Baptist de La Salle
Meditation #187.2 St. – Charles Borromeo, Patron Saint of the Arts

Imagine . . . find a quiet moment at some point, close your eyes . . . and allow your mind to imaginatively wander into the various offices and rooms throughout De La Salle North Catholic High School.

Consider your colleagues and the work they do . . . how in each encircled realm, there are differing tasks and differing pressures: how there are 8th Graders to inspire, there are bills to pay, new jobs to gain and current jobs to keep, donors to befriend and ask, food to prepare, students to teach polynomial functions or titrations or bicameral government, athletes to teach how to manage setbacks or humbly embrace success, families to listen to and counsel, machines to repair, a building to heat and clean, phone calls to return, community resources to marshal, lessons to plan, meetings to prepare for, and, well, the work goes ever on, a breadth and variety and tonality virtually infinite in scope. It can seem a cacophony, especially with teenagers.

But . . . in our quiet, creative and hopeful imagining . . . we might sense the stuttering complementarity of it, perhaps not always sweetly melodic, for in our work we are so near to some notes and quite distant from others . . . we rarely hear them all come together.

To that end . . . at some time this week, take ten minutes – just ten – and walk through our beloved school with an empathic ear keen for the symphony that is our cumulative work.

Dec 15 – 19, 2014

1 message   Sun, Dec 14, 2014 at 8:11 PM

"How long has Jesus been knocking at the door of your heart, waiting to enter?"

St. John Baptist de La Salle
Meditation 85.1 – on the vigil of the Nativity

Advent and Christmastide are seasons of the divine entering our lives— the Word made Flesh—all in the multifarious ways we may understand this mystery. Three centuries ago in Reims, France, De La Salle spoke directly to his young Brothers about their Catholic faith. Now in 2014 . . . and in Portland . . . what is that knocking, that incessant knocking? Sometimes, we just wish it would stop.

Monday morning, we start week 16. In these first two weeks of December, three students have transferred out, seniors falter every day; we've scheduled a number of family meetings this week so all parties know where they stand before the break; a percentage of students have made no progress at all; our first data set from student writing is cause for despair as about 10% earned a proficiency score; a few students consistently arrive late to school; students don't complete homework, don't read the assigned material, balk in committing to participate, and may be surly when corrected. Many teeter on confidence's wobbly ledge.

One might turn away in a kind of professional grief. *It is too much; I cannot bear the weight of it.* And then . . . there's that knocking . . . Jeremiah wrote about this over two and a half millennia earlier, how we wish to not hear the knock, to not heed the voice, to turn from our heart's call: "If I say, 'I will not mention him or speak any more in his name,' there is in my heart as it were a burning fire shut up in my bones. I am weary from holding it in; indeed, I cannot."[29]

Joseph Campbell (The *Hero with a Thousand Faces*, 1949) claims that the hero's great act is not so much to triumph but to submit. Answering a call means opening the door to a mystery . . . and, in faith, stepping through to embrace the desiccating day-to-dayness of it, what De La Salle described as being "imperceptibly led." There on the wobbly ledge with our students, we are a collective holiness they cling to.

---

[29] Jeremiah 20:9

Nov 30 – Dec 4, 2015

1 message   Sun, Nov 29, 2015 at 8:09 PM

"Because you have to prepare the hearts of others for the coming of Jesus Christ, you must first of all dispose your own hearts to be entirely filled with zeal, in order to render your words effective in those whom you instruct."

St. John Baptist de La Salle
Meditations 2.1 – Second Sunday of Advent

As the earth spun on its axis through this day, a billion Christians, each within a longitudinal strip of a time zone, lit the first Advent candle, a small light in a great darkness. So begins the sweeping, renewing metaphor of Jesus as the light of the world. Set aside what we know of Saturnalia and winter solstice festivals . . . this light is the One we warm ourselves to, tend to, and live by.

Today's reading from Luke[30] speaks of tumult in the heavens, "on earth nations will be in dismay, perplexed." It's a passage fraught with prophetic, symbolic language of imminent, terrifying change. Consider for a moment the stern challenge Jesus issues to his followers – get your lives in order, quit fussing about small things, do not let your heart "become drowsy . . . be vigilant at all times . . . and pray that you have the strength to escape the tribulations that are imminent." The slow illumination toward Jesus' birth reveals a troubled and chaotic place . . . not unlike the corner of Lombard and Interstate[31] at dawn or dusk.

Only a strong heart While there is light, it will not benignly shine on
can instruct. lollipops and butterflies and everywhere people
hugging each other. De La Salle's call to "dispose

---

[30] Luke 21:25-28, 34-36
[31] Location of De La Salle North Catholic High School until August 2021.

80

our own hearts" is the order of the days ahead. Our world alight in truth requires, then, that our own lives be ordered, that we are vigilant to our mission task . . . none of which is possible without our hearts "entirely filled with zeal." Cast a light into the closed and guarded lives of our students, and only a strong heart can instruct. When you greet a student, you instruct; when you pass a student in the hallway and nod at her, you instruct; when you call their parent, you instruct; when two or more of you gather to lift up a stumbled or stumbling student, you instruct.

All true, but only partly true.

When you greet your colleague, you instruct; when you toss a "how can I help?" to another department, you instruct; when you note the somber stirrings of a colleague, you instruct.

The staff of De La Salle North Catholic is WE. If we cannot be a WE, this school cannot fulfill its mission. Our students are transformed because, first, *we are transformed* . . . our faithful Community is the Lasallian charism that renders our words so effectively in those whom we instruct.

Dec 2 – 6, 2020
1 message   Sun, Dec 1, 2019 at 7:44 PM

"Let us then throw off the works of darkness and put on the armor of light."

Romans 13:12

The four weeks of Advent are a time of reflection and hope. Christians around the world go inward and raise a question: am I prepared for God in my life?

This is as a big a question as any. Back in the day, Jesus famously asked his disciples, who do people say that I am? His disciples replied, well, people say a lot of things. What followed was a thing Jesus did a lot . . . he made it personal. As the story goes, Jesus listened patiently as his disciples rattled off a list of "things people said." Then, getting personal, Jesus said, "who do *you* say that I am?"

It's a question that requires some introspection. How we live is one way we answer it.

We call it Advent because we're on the cusp of an arrival. Within the Catholic Church, this Sunday marks the beginning of the liturgical year— a year's sequence of storytelling that enumerates God's salvific story. We call it Advent because we're on the cusp of an arrival, a story of light and promise and a transcendent question. It's one of the reasons we light a candle each week, lengthening light as the darkness deepens.

I've always embraced the irony of Advent . . . we prepare for a season when people first see a great light juxtaposed against a time when daylight recedes to its lowest ebb. The cross currents of 'great light' and 'least light' call up a ritual of hope, what St. Paul was referring to in his letter to the people of Rome; "Put on the armor of light." What are ya gonna do? In the face of difficulty, you put up a fight.

Let's face these three weeks ahead straight on . . . counseling business is manic right now; we're talking with students all this and next week about attendance and passing classes and staying on track for graduation; seniors juggle homework and work and college applications and home life; and students scramble to repair grades or complete work. We're all running out of days. We're in the Lasallian push of that "human and Christian education."

What shall be our armor of light? Let *us* be a source of light for our students, for our families, and for each other.

Nov 30 – Dec 4, 2020
1 message   Sun, Nov 29, 2020 at 9:27 PM

"The night is advanced; the day is at hand."

Romans 13:11

On Monday there are exactly nine hours of daylight but decreasing about a minute a day over the next three weeks. We've been feeling it, seeing it, knowing it in a way that gets inside us. More than earth's axial tilt as we move to the winter solstice, the darkness we feel flows from our separateness; we must work so hard to fight it off, to sustain our community's union, our "precious gem."

To symbolize our faith in *God-with-us* amid a darkening time, we light a candle.

Advent reminds us to retell the story, to start the Jesus story again, to prepare ourselves for the work ahead. We are coming into the hardest time of the school year, when—even in typical years—our students find the work harder to do than it was in September, so much more at stake, so many more impediments. To lift our students, to be the big sisters and big brothers to the students in our care, only our *zeal* for them and for our community can lift us; and, as De La Salle reminded his young Brothers, *zeal is an act of faith.*

This shows up in the many ways we already know about—how we plan, how we greet and work with our students, how we collaborate, how we reach out to the students who seem, as De La Salle often said, "very far from salvation." We see what is good in them, see the light in them, and call that best part of them forward.

In this season of reflection and preparation, *in faith and with zeal,* we pre-pare ourselves and step into the work. In this third term, let's extend our collective reach to the students furthest from us.

When we do this, light brightens, and the day is at hand.

Dec 5 – 9, 2022
1 message   Sun, Dec 5, 2022 at 8:49 PM

"For the students entrusted to our care."

St. John Baptist de La Salle

I've wondered about this phrase for a long time. It shows up everywhere in De La Salle's writings, his letters, his *Meditations*. What happened over time, of course, is the phrase morphed into a Lasallian meme . . . and now, maybe, a Lasallian cliché.

I've read straight through that phrase hundreds of times, enough to think less of it. But recently, I put it alongside a different phrase: "the students assigned to my class." This juxtaposition surprised me. Swapping in "entrusted" and "care" elevated both words. Being *assigned* is something an institutional algorithm can do; being *entrusted* is something only we can do. And *class* is a place, whereas *care* is an action, one that requires virtue.

So, who's doing the "entrusting"? De La Salle frequently noted that the students are "entrusted to you by pastors, by fathers and mothers"; sometimes, those students "are the ones entrusted to you by God." In this way, teaching becomes a sacramental undertaking.

And "care" reaches down into my gut, roils me, keeps me awake at night, exhorts me to do better.

For us this Second Week of Advent, our *spiritual practice* is to answer the sacred call of being *entrusted to care* for our students, in the only way we can, "with an ardent zeal."

God bless you all in your beautiful work.

Dec 12 – 16, 2022

1 message   Sun, Dec 11, 2022 at 8:09 PM

"Strengthen the hands that are feeble,
Make firm the knees that are weak,
say to those whose hearts are frightened:
Be strong, fear not!
Here is your God."

Isaiah 35:3-4

When we drive to school, it's dark.

Out of the car, and it's 36°, an atmospheric river flowing overhead, wind throwing rain in your face as you dash up the stairs, flailing for your key as it waggles away from you at the end of the lanyard. *BzzzzT.* The front door unlocks. Warmth and light.

In.

The phone at the Front Desk flickers with messages. Shadows cloak the courtyard. Bones creak. Muscles nag. The coffee's on, and a few stand nearby, mugs dangling from fingers. An arm stretch, a neck roll. There's chatter about the weekend, benign background noise, as eyes flick to the coffee flow, its earthy emanation fills the air. Elsewhere, lesson plans open on laptops, the copy machine clicks and buzzes, emitting math problems, short stories, chemistry equations. Emails fill inboxes. Drivers gather, check routes and names. Staff throw themselves in from outside, flap their coats, spraying water across the carpet. All through the school, work lists open on desktops. There's the phone ringing again.

They're coming.

Some awake for 90 minutes or more, already on a bus; some are sleepy, others only hear the weekend's commotion, a loud noise in their head. They're stepping into the morning's weather, climbing into a car, clutching a backpack.

They're coming.

Out the car and bus windows, the early darkness and the steady *ssshhh* of tires in the rain wakens some, lulls others. A face leans on the rear window; eyes open wide to the traffic lights and brake lights and streetlights mottled by the rain running sideways along the car's window. A yawn. Hundreds of yawns.

They're coming.

Buses kneel at the Killingsworth stop and students flip up their hoods, raise their shoulders and hold the hood flap against the wind. They're jogging. In both lanes on 42nd, cars alternate turning right, turning left into the pull-up lane. Going. Stopping. Going.

They're coming.

Up the steps, a few take two at a time. The wind flings the rain against the front door. Some light illuminates the clouds, but not much; shadows recede, but not all. Students fill hallways, step across thresholds into classrooms and offices, faces glisten from the rain.

It's 7:45 AM. They're here, and more are coming.

You believe something, and that belief wakes you up early, drives you to school in the dark, pours your coffee, readies your van, preps your room, straightens your office. Every morning, you are preparing the way, filling valleys, lowering mountains . . . because at De La Salle North Catholic, every morning is Advent.

Dec 4 – 8, 2023

1 message   Sun, Dec 3, 2023 at 8:20 PM

"Strengthen the hands that are feeble,
make firm the knees that are weak,
say to those whose hearts are frightened,
Be strong, fear not!"

Isaiah 35:3

The bland bleakness of a hopeless world seems to stretch out to the edges of our known world; pick your social ill or global grief. All of it streaming right to our palm, every day, without ceasing . . . benumbed, we tap a headline and then another and another; soon, rapturously enfeebled by it all, our knees grow weak, and fear grows for everything and everyone we hold dear.

This, and beneath the grayscape of our weekend rains and interminable cloud cover, one longs for light.

It may be small and perilously close to going out . . . but the light of Advent's first candle signals hope. And a call to act.

Let's remember the *why of our calling* . . . turn   *Make strong what is*
our attention inward, to family, to colleagues,   *nearest at hand.*
to our beloved Lasallian school. Not to ig-
nore the world at large, but to make strong what is nearest at hand—our collective capacity to touch the hearts and teach the minds of the students confided to our care.

"Be strong, fear not!" There's more light coming.

⊕   ⊕   ⊕

"How long has Jesus been knocking at the door of your heart, waiting to enter?"

St. John Baptist de La Salle
Meditation 85.1 - for the Vigil of the Nativity of Jesus Christ

Okay, maybe it's a little early to strum the nativity chord, this being just the Second Sunday of Advent. Then, again, Advent does mean "to arrive." To show up. You know, someone knocking at your door. The four weeks of Advent are about the wait and the preparation, the lead up to that pounding on the door called the Vigil on Christmas Eve.

De La Salle's 85th meditation opens with Joseph and Mary needing to leave Nazareth, on account of an edict from Emperor Augustus ordering a census, and travel to Bethlehem (cue Luke 2:1-7). There, they wander house to house, to inns, knocking on doors; but none would take them in. Bethlehem had closed its doors to them.

Recent times (pick your timeframe . . . they all work) have toughened us a bit, made us wary, cautious, if not quick to close up.

Give it a moment . . . in your own life, *what have you closed off?*

I must admit that I don't want to admit that I've done this, but . . . well, y'know . . .

Enter the stories and songs of Advent which tell us to "level the mountains, fill in the valleys, prepare the way." In a way, we are akin to that distant town of Bethlehem, and every day students come into our school. Whenever a student crosses a threshold into your classroom or office, it is a "knocking at the door of your heart." Have you prepared the way . . . are you ready to open the door?

Many blessings to all for the beautiful work you carry out every day.

Reflecting on December's Lasallian Meme

> "How long has Jesus been knocking at the door of your heart, waiting to enter?"
>
> St. John Baptist de La Salle
> *Meditation 85.1 – For the Vigil of the Nativity of Jesus Christ*

De La Salle met with Adrien Nyel, someone soliciting help from him. Initially, he was not receptive but opened his home to Nyel for more conversations. About a month later, they opened the first Lasallian school in Saint-Maurice.

Choose a prompt to write about

➤ December is a time of year that we often want to close our door, get some work done, take a breath. But students need you. Write about this protective tendency and what you and your team can do to support both you and others, especially your students.

➤ Write about an issue emerging for you in this fourth month; then, consider it through this Lasallian meme of being open and available to students and each other. How can you or your team creatively answer the knock at the door?

January

act with love and true zeal

January

"You must not doubt that it is a great gift of God . . . to be entrusted with the instruction of children. Let it be clear, then, in all your relations with the students entrusted to you that you act with love and true zeal."

St. John Baptist de La Salle
Meditations for the Time of Retreat, 9.1

January is a lot . . . the semester's end when everyone in the school reviews the first semester and simultaneously prepares for the second. Anxiety and uncertainty grip many: instructional plans may not have panned out and need revision; academic goals rest on high-stakes exams; the mid-year flux can vex and overwhelm everyone in a school.

In this fifth visitation De La Salle is 29 years old and is on his way home, walking in the countryside under a gentle snowfall. He's thinking about his schools and teachers when the snow intensifies, and winds pick up. What was calming now threatens; he's disoriented and tumbles into a snowbank. Subject to hypothermia and wondering if this might be it for him, he struggles to get out.

How do we keep going when going seems futile?

Every year, there's at least one big moment when the typical effort is not enough; sometimes, even an all-out effort is not enough, the moment too big, never seen before.

At some point each year, teachers and staff face exhaustion and occasional bouts of futility. It's your *ceaseless why* that keeps you going.

In the Champagne Countryside
Outside Reims, Winter, 1681

From April to September 1679, Père De La Salle and Adrien Nyel opened three schools[32]; and students flocked to them. However, in a few months' time, troubling reports surfaced: the young teachers were, at best, unprepared; at worst, illiterate or abusive. From fall 1679 to winter 1681, De La Salle worked with the teachers to establish a community that would foster good order in the schools. His efforts, however, were not enough. He was unsure what to do next.

Shortly after New Year's 1681, De La Salle travelled to the Champagne countryside on family business, but he was preoccupied with the schools. A few days later, he started on his return trip to Reims just as snow began to fall. He was prepared, dressed in boots, long coat, scarf, hat, and gloves. The slow-falling snow felt bright, calming; he'd be home in a few hours. Shortly into his trek home, however, the weather changed; the bucolic snowfall turned dangerous.

Even though snow had been falling intermittently since morning and the abbey was more than hospitable, De La Salle had been gone long enough.

"Wait another day," the abbot said.

De La Salle was restive for home. He thanked the abbot and started out for Reims. An hour into his travel, he saw it; it was getting worse. As he walked, clouds darkened, snow fell heavier, an unexpected gust blew off his hat so that he had to chase ahead a few strides to retrieve it. *Thank God, I'm halfway home*, he thought, *I'll be there in an hour.*

The cold conjured a memory of a conversation with Père Dorigny[33] about the teachers at Saint Maurice. It was a clear fall night, almost winter. Dorigny had come to his home, the two of them dining next to the hearth. Dorigny dropped his elbows on the table, shoulders hunched, as he daubed his bread in the au jus.

---

[32] Schools opened in the parishes of Saint-Maurice, Saint-Jacques, and Saint-Symphorien, all in Reims.
[33] Nicolas Dorigny was pastor of Saint-Maurice, the first school De La Salle opened.

"Mon frere," he tells De La Salle. "I am concerned about the school and the teachers." De La Salle remembers the look in Dorigny's eyes, looking up at him from across the table, a yeasty crumb on his lip.

"Last week alone, two teachers walked out of their classrooms, yesterday Monsieur Faubert never showed up . . . kids were outside, shouting at neighbors."

De La Salle pulled up his collar, held it fast with his right hand. The snow was falling harder now, drifting against any rise, a tree, a bush. The memory of Dorigny at his home flickered, then sharpened.

"It seemed a good idea, these schools of yours," Dorigny says. "But, mon frère, I'm afraid you are in over your head."

De La Salle cringed at this memory. Another gust surprised him, the snow prickly against his face. He closed his eyes. Some snow skittered in behind his collar. He tightened his scarf, held his hat with his gloved hand, and turned his face from the gusts—his jaw hardened, his lips felt numb.

He looked up. Ahead, it was all suddenly unfamiliar. The landmarks he knew by rote had changed; void of color and dimension, the rapid snowfall was transforming the landscape into a formless whiteout. He stood still, looked up and back, and then kept on. A few steps later, his left foot flooped through the snow and planted lower than his right; shocked and off-center, his imbalance threw him left, and he stretched out an arm, certain he'd catch himself, but the snow had banked against the ravine wall making the road seem wider than it actually was, and he wheeled over twice, coming to with a throb in his head, everything dark, snow in his mouth, cold against his eyes, his left arm behind him, one leg bent.

The world muted, suspended. He pushed with a leg and winced. Melting snow dribbled into his ear, and he flinched. Swallowing was hard. He realized his head was a little lower than his feet. He struggled to orient himself. *How far am I from home?*

His legs were chilled and hands stung. Panic pulsed through him. And the prophet's words came to him: "My word is like the snow . . .

that comes down from the sky."[34]

So, is this it?

Snow had slipped into his shoes; snowmelt circled his legs. He struggled to bend his fingers. His right leg was numb, so he pushed from his hip. Stuck. With his right side immobile, he used his left foot . . . the push extended his hands, and he thrust his shoulders up and felt the open air with his left hand.

His center shifted, a bit up and then down. Just then, something opened beneath him, an air pocket he popped when he straightened his leg, and he dropped, snow falling atop him as he clawed to hold on the surface. Covered again. His right leg felt useless, and he could not gain leverage with his left – his arms tangled around his head. He gulped snow, gasped. Sweating, a rivulet rolled down his ribs and he shivered.

He reached up and pushed some snow aside while he also stretched his left leg, pulled it in then pushed it a different direction when it struck some solid-something. . . and his right hand grabbed a branch, a push and a pull all at one. He moved, gathered himself and pushed again. Then kept going.

Each of De La Salle's biographers, in varying degrees, recounts this "near-death experience" that left him with physical and psychic scars. As Blain notes, De La Salle "finally managed to escape, but the accident left him with a rupture caused by the violent efforts he had made to save his life."[35]

Safely home, time passes. During Holy Week that spring, De La Salle brought the teachers to live with him at his house where he could coach them on teaching and counsel them on communal life.

---

[34] Isaiah 55:10-11
[35] Blain, Jean-Baptiste. *The Life of John Baptist de La Salle.* Volume One, p 77.

Jan 22 – 25, 2013
1 message   Sun, Jan 21, 2013 at 8:57 PM

"Do you look upon the good that you are trying to achieve in [your students] as the foundation of all the good that they will practice for the rest of their lives? The habits of virtue that are cultivated during youth encounter less resistance from selfishness and form the deepest roots in the heart."

St. John Baptist De La Salle
Meditation for the Time of Retreat, 2.1

In the January 2013 edition of the *Harvard Education Letter*, Laura Pappano[36] provides a narrative of recent work on "so-called performance character traits." Specifically, she talks about research on "grit." She interviewed teachers, students and researchers; and while the idea of "teaching grit" remains an open question, there is no doubt that making students aware of their own "grit score" and marshaling successes in areas of handling setbacks or working through obstacles can have a salutary effect on student achievement.

Struggle and frustration are the byproducts of a grappling, reaching intellect. We ask our students to do a lot more than their peers at other schools. And for most, their education has not prepared them for it . . . so they may likely be frustrated and perhaps fail at some of it. How, then, do we prepare them to know that these events are a natural "part of learning and not a sign of failure"? Struggle and frustration are the byproducts of a grappling, reaching intellect.

---

[36] Pappano, Laura. 'Grit' and the new character education. *Harvard Education Letter* (Volume 29, Number 1). January/February 2013.

Pappano's article taps on the spirit of De La Salle. The work you do every day—with generosity and zeal—helps your students build "habits of virtue" that they will "practice for the rest of their lives." Our own perseverance in instructing them can be a powerful message of our love and hope for them.

Keep going!

Jan 6 – 10, 2014
1 message   Sun, Jan 5, 2014 at 8:07 PM

"Often remind yourself that you are in the Presence of God."

St. John Baptist de La Salle
Letter #3 – to a young Brother, 1701

Happy New Year!

With the Feast of Epiphany, we hear the story of the Magi come to visit the Child, but not before conferring with King Herod, who "was greatly troubled." One can hear the drippy unctuous voice of Herod, "Search diligently for the child . . . bring me word, that I too may . . . do him homage." Right. However we take this story into our hearts, there resides in that exchange a reminder that even amid revelation, there is risk. "Do not be afraid," were the words of the Heavenly Voices. I must admit, though, that fear sometimes operates ferociously in my life, surging through me amid my worries. In this 1701 letter, De La Salle further remonstrates with the Brother about being preoccupied with his "state of life," the source of his unrest. Hence, De La Salle's exhortation.

So . . . when we start our day . . . and we start each class . . . and as we start this New Year . . . with "Let us remember that we are in the Holy Presence of God," let's imagine it as a call to courage, our faith as a bulwark against our fears. In such a Presence, what wonders might we together accomplish?

As 2013 counted down, I did wonder about the people in my life, the work I do, the garden I tend. I looked through the transparencies of my past as if staring into a layered pond, clarity to some depth here, murky there. Scenes floated up and then dissipated. How many writers remind us that the past is like that, is not even really past? Its whisper a nag in my ear.

Huh? What is Tim saying?

This . . . for 2014, let's be a community that engages the present as it looks ahead . . . let's forgo the "what if's" of the past; look to the possible, to the doable, to the solutions we need to make De La Salle North Catholic the school our students need.

⊕ ⊕ ⊕

Jan 19 – 22, 2016
1 message   Sun, Jan 18, 2016 at 7:07 PM

"Do not be troubled about the present or disquieted about the future but be concerned only about the moment that you must now live."

St. John Baptist de La Salle
Meditation on Mt 6:26-34

I am writing this day from a small room in the Aloysius hut at St. Joseph's Camp in Duncan Mills, CA, alongside the Russian River where Kim and I spent a weekend with 34 senior boys on the Called and Chosen Retreat, a time for discerning the vocational call whispering inside them. The boys hail from Lasallian schools in Los Angeles, Sacramento, Yakima, Concord, Tucson, Napa, San Francisco, Milwaukie, and Portland.

It is an impressive thing, no doubt, to sit among them in a ring under the chapel's steep-ceiling and listen to their questions, to their wishes, to their worries. Our seniors carry some mighty big questions about their next year, as well as what's out there after college, a path through many decades. When they turn my age, it will be 2057.

They carry these worries with courage, for they don't have to look too far to see what may befall them. Among neighbors or friends or within their families are the scars of lives gone awry. We see this displayed in each countdown to graduation when excitement masks the accumulating worry of being away from friends, away from family, and on their own in a disinterested world. All of this underscores the core mission of our school—the faith formation of the young people in our care. In every moment of students' lives at our school, they are near God's grace, near our care to which they are confided.

I ask you all to take courage in your role and to be gentle.

Jan 9 – 13, 2017

1 message   Sun, Jan 8, 2017 at 6:16 PM

"If you want the instructions you give those whom you teach to be effective in drawing them to the practice of good, you must practice these truths yourself. It is zeal which makes your students capable of receiving a share in the grace which is in you for doing good."

St. John Baptist de La Salle
Meditation for The Time of Retreat, 2.3

Ice and snow notwithstanding, the last few weeks of school have seen a marked increase in students in counseling and administrative offices. None of this ought to surprise any of us, as this surge of anxiety and acting out typically coincides with the holidays and the imminent exams. We know it's coming. When it happens, we know the catalysts are deep, something a young person may not want to admit, may not want to say aloud, even to someone they love and respect.

The Lasallian charism of faith and zeal bears these moments in a particular way. It is normative that students will err, will occasionally be unable to manage their everyday pressures, perhaps more so our beautiful and fragile students. Three centuries ago, De La Salle wrote about the "burdens that often overwhelm" a student. For this very reason, "God has had the goodness to remedy so great a misfortune" with compassionate and faith-filled adults such as you.

Our students call De La Salle North Catholic "family" because you do what makes this school a blessing in their lives—when life's pressures bear down on them, you support them; if need be, correct them and draw them "to the practice of good." In all cases, speak and act in such a way that touches their hearts, not despite their frailty but because of it.

Jan 23 – 27, 2017
1 message   Sun, Jan 22, 2017 at 7:32 PM

"Just as God is the one who gives light to everyone who comes into the world, God also gives light to the spirit of your students and leads them to love and to practice the good that you teach them."

St. John Baptist de La Salle
Meditation for Time of Retreat, 3.3

Admittedly, this is sometimes hard to see, and therefore also harder to believe . . . students' response to our work with them emerges from God's spirit. But this is one of the core elements of De La Salle's faith, that one is to see teaching children "through the eyes of faith." It is the reason his great *Meditations* continues to reverberate across centuries: everything about that moment, everything that leads to that moment, from the community that sustains the Brothers, to the families that nurture the students, to the myriad instructional moments that occur through a day in a school . . . these are understood, in the eyes of faith, as having arisen within Providence. Sacred. Purposeful. A source of one's salvation.

In our understanding, then, that each child—and each moment with that child—presents as God emerging in our mission field: here, be gentle, teach, love, correct, persist. In the Lasallian world, this is how we work ourselves toward God. Or, rather, how God enables us to work toward God.

And it is why community—how we are together, how we are with each other, and how we present as one to our students—*resides at the center of everything we do* . . . we are to be the model of the possible Human Family, the solidarity of God's One Family, what succeeds when the world around us founders. None of this can be done separate from others here, but only as we apply ourselves to our community in faith and love.

104

Seeing us in this way, our students and families come to know that God's love pervades all things. Through De La Salle's eyes of faith, we attain our "salvation personally by a union of our will with the will of God." In our Catholic story, we do not believe that we just got a job at De La Salle North Catholic. No. Rather, we believe that God chose us, at this particular time . . . to work with these particular students.

Jan 2 – 5, 2018
1 message   Sun, Jan 1, 2018 at 7:54 PM

"God diffuses the fragrance of divine knowledge throughout the world by human ministers."

St. John Baptist de La Salle
Meditations for the Time of Retreat, 1.1

It is well documented that early Christendom aligned the liturgical year with the astronomical year, suffusing a broadly understood natural phenomenon with a nascent divine one. And, so, Jesus' birth aligns closely with the winter solstice, heralding six months of increasing light. This time of year, we often come to school in the dark and leave in the dark. More light would be great.

Problem is, it's a slow start to more light, just about a minute a day as the earth continues its elliptic around the sun; in about a week, the rate of more light per day will increase to about two to three minutes a day. I mention this oh-so-slow change just as our school embarks on a critical year. At times of challenge, it is best to keep close to foundational things—teach, counsel, exhort, love, believe in the power of our work and the "precious gem" of our community. One keeps at the good work to keep the good work going. In time, light is everywhere.

Today I read about poet Jane Kenyon (1947–1995) and an essay she wrote called "Everything I Know About Writing Poetry." Amid all the New Year's resolutions and howtochangeyourlife lists that showed up today, hers stood out. I offer it as something worth hearing and taking to heart:

> *Be a good steward of your gifts. Protect your time. Feed your inner life. Avoid too much noise. Read good books, have good sentences*

*in your ears. Be by yourself as often as you can. Walk. Take the
phone off the hook.*

As the story unfolds, Jesus—the Light of the World—was born at least
light. And we've never been the same.

iStock

Jan 6 – 10, 2020
1 message   Sun, Jan 5, 2020 at 7:45 PM

"Fulfill your ministry with all the affection of your heart."

St. John Baptist de La Salle
Meditations for the Time of Retreat, 9.1

Pick your New Year's metaphor . . . more daylight each day, first baby of the new decade, Janus, a distant horizon, resolutions, discovery, epiphany, the Magi.

Me? I've been thinking about my yard. Imagining the rain seeping, sweetly seeping to the roots of my cover crop (sown in November), each tiny branch root sending tendrils (forming still more branch roots) through the soil to absorb moisture and spur leafy growth. Up now about 4", they'll double in height as they leaf out . . . turning them under later this spring returns nutrients and breaks down the Joy garden's dense clay soil. Sowing Portland Nursery's "green manure" in the fall teaches me a lot about ministry. The effort-to-yield relationship is not linear (two beds are thriving, a third is okay, a fourth is barren). It's all a dad-blame test of my patience!

The more challenging the moment, the more affection we need to carry it out.

We return this week to our ministerial work . . . with our students and families, and with each other. The "with each other" starts right away on Monday morning. We can only do this work if our community is strong, "a precious gem" St. La Salle called it. January 6 to June 6 . . . Retreat to Graduation . . . a five-month act of communal promise, hope, and love. Little of what we do ever reveals itself right away. Every bit of what we do is a test of patience, an act of faith, something we must do with all the affection of our hearts. The deal with affection in a school community, especially as the year waxes on, is that when it is most needed, it may be most difficult to muster. The more challenging the moment, the more affection we need to carry on. But this is our ministry . . . the affection of our hearts open to one another and to our students . . . in this act, we fulfill our ministry.

I miss you all and look forward to being with you again. It's 2020, a big year for our beloved school.

Jan 4 – 8, 2021
1 message   Sun, Jan 3, 2021 at 8:20 PM

"Let it be clear, then, in all your relations with the students entrusted to you that you . . . act with love and true zeal."

St. John Baptist de La Salle
Meditations for the Time of Retreat, 9.1

One of the reasons we "remember that we are in the Holy Presence of God" is how that full stop we take prepares our hearts. In that quiet remembrance, we contemplate the sacredness of our work. Sure, it doesn't seem terribly sacred when what we occasionally see are tops of heads, avatars, or yawning students. But it is. We call our students to the moment, as we also marshal our own moral and professional capacity to meet them, counsel them, teach them.

Here we are, back to school in the home stretch of Semester One. We have done so well because we met the struggle together, saw the sincere effort in each other, lifted each other, and cheered each other on this unprecedented journey. It's our community strength that enables us to support our students and families.

This is our work this year . . . to look upon our community and our work through the "eyes of faith" and commit to care for and sustain each other so that we can – with "zeal" – instruct the students and families entrusted to our care.

Let's embrace every blessed thing about the collective work this year . . . what works and what doesn't work, our students who thrive and our students who fail; be ready to lift and haul and carry and bless each other . . . it's how we fix what needs fixing, carry on, and—in so doing—love our students.

Jan 11 – 15, 2021
1 message   Sun, Jan 11, 2021 at 8:35 PM

On January 6, 2021, American citizens stormed the US Capitol, shattered windows, broke down doors, assaulted Capitol Police, stole documents, and occupied offices and the main chamber, causing the Senate and the House to temporarily shutter its certification of the 2020 Presidential election. Dozens were injured, including Capitol police, and five people died.

"Remembering that God is with you will help and inspire you in all that you do."

St. John Baptist de La Salle
May 15, 1701, earliest existing letter of the Founder to a Brother

It already seems—does it not?—that last Sunday is somehow part of a much more distant past, part of a separate age, so shocking were the events of January 6 that the arrow of time was plucked from its flight, and we entered an alternate, out-of-time dimension. So, what we did last Monday was, like, how long ago? Can you remember what we did?

January 6, the Feast of the Epiphany, manifests light breaking through darkness, the magi come to Mary and Joseph's humble setting to recognize, and pay homage to, the Christ Child, Emmanuel, God with us. It was seeing with "the eyes of faith" and acting with "true zeal."

If ever there were a time to recall the purpose of our work, it is now in front of us. And do what? In a time of grief or calamity, do good work.

Let's step forward into this week, be among our students and colleagues, and remember that all we do is conducted in the Holy Presence of God.

On the eve of the Chinese New Year, a gunman opened fire in a Los Angeles nightclub where Asian Americans had gathered to celebrate the Lunar New Year, stoking national fears rooted in racism and rising rates of violence.

"People tend to be afraid of what they don't understand."

Venus Sun
Director of Culture and Community Engagement
Lan Su Chinese Garden in Portland, Oregon

Today's Google Doodle celebrates the opening of the Lunar New Year, the year of the Rabbit.

Today's headline, however, is a nightmare.

Tragedy made coming together all that more important. The terrible events that unfolded in Los Angeles over the last 24 hours sent shock waves of grief and fear through Asian American communities across the country. With security heightened, celebrations nationwide carried on. Here in Portland, attendees at the Lan Su Chinese Garden celebration noted that "the tragedy made coming together all that more important."

We are living amid a tense and tender time, our wounds and fear close to the surface, but we go on living . . . not cowed, but embracing our Lasallian work to welcome all, to assure students and families, everyone associated with De La Salle North Catholic that you can come here, that you belong.

112

In the everydayness of our halls and classrooms and offices, this is a high stress week; the timelines in everyone's work are taut: students with grades astride passing or failing, seniors studying feverishly to secure the best mark for the vital 7th Semester, admin hiring an English teacher to be in a classroom in a week, Admissions helping interested transfer students close the deal . . . everyone's list just a bit too long.

It's all so much . . . the far-away and the right-here of every day. Even so, tomorrow and the day after, and the day after that, and all the days to June 9, we'll come together, ready to receive and care for our students. As Venus Sun reflected on the tragic news, "it's a moment for us to realize that we are needed here."

Reflecting on January's Lasallian Meme

> "You must not doubt that it is a great gift of God. . . to be entrusted with the instruction of children. Let it be clear, then, in all your relations with the students entrusted to you that you act with love and true zeal."
>
> St. John Baptist de La Salle
> *Meditations for the Time of Retreat, 9.1*

De La Salle had been travelling in the Champagne District in winter 1691. He started home for Reims amid a light snowfall. As he neared home, his mind reeled from the troubles awaiting him. Suddenly, he found himself in a whiteout, disoriented, then pitched into a snowbank.

Choose a prompt to write about

➢ Consider a time in your year when your efforts seemed futile, when you were not the difference-maker you had envisioned. How did you keep going? On whom did you lean?

➢ Write about a challenging issue emerging for you in this fifth month—the midpoint in the year. Then, consider it through this Lasallian meme of being "entrusted." How do you and your team revitalize the trusted relationship so that you can "act with love and true zeal?"

February

have much patience

February

"Accept with much patience the difficulties you have to suffer."

St. John Baptist de La Salle
Meditations for the Time of Retreat, 9.1

Dark, cold, bundled against winter, nested, reaching for the covers, inert.

After the long hours of January reading papers, evaluating semester exams, and then planning for Semester 2, changes emerge, ever so slight though they may be. For a few weeks this month, students' energy falls off . . . the long push to finish Semester 1 exhausts just about everyone.

In this sixth visitation, De La Salle, now 31, is confronted by his long-trusted teachers, the Brothers who've stood by him for years and who have endured the charged conditions of a startup enterprise.

Why should we expect to suffer difficulties?

This mid-year month finds us at a tipping point, and we wonder if we can weather the challenges ahead. Nurturing our communal trust and respect as we care for each other will keep us going and will redound to the students in our care.

⊕ ⊕ ⊕

The House on Rue Neuve
Reims, Early Fall, 1682

On June 24, 1682, a reconstituted community of schoolteachers and Père De La Salle moved into a rented property on Rue Neuve – adjoining houses, a chapel, and courtyards where the fledgling group might establish new norms for their community. It was a time of expansion for the small society, still not well known to the public, but enjoying a rising reputation among the pastors in and around Reims. Over an eight-month span, from March through October of 1682, De La Salle opened four schools in outlying towns near Reims.

The new schools stretched community resources. The teachers could see it showing up in their daily lives, fewer school supplies, meager meals, and they worried about the association's future, as well as their own. So, this one Fall evening, as the teachers were on their evening constitutional in Reims, one of them brought it up.

Thursday afternoon, clouds streaming from the north, winds rattling the trees, and there were the Brothers, paired up, walking soberly on the cobbled street, bundled against what looked to be rain coming their way.

"Brother Henri," said Nicolas.[37] "I need to say something."

Henri[38] turned to him as they both kept walking down rue Neuve; he spoke calmly, almost a whisper, holding up an open palm. "Silence, Brother. We are to be quiet now."

"*Oui.*" Nicolas's head bobbed and then straightened. He rubbed his face. His stomach seized but kept pace with Henri. Behind them, their Brothers followed, a few held small, black-bound books with red and purple ribbons marking their place in the Psalms or St. Paul's letters.

---

[37] Nicolas Vuyart, one of the three (with Gabriel Drolin and De La Salle) who proclaimed a Vow of Association in 1691. He had joined the teaching community prior to the move to the Neuve property and was well respected among the community.
[38] Henri L'Heureux joined the teaching group before the rue Neuve move. In the 1688 First Chapter, he was selected by the community, and endorsed by De La Salle, to be the new Superior. See Loes, Augustine, FSC. *The First De La Salle Brothers.*

Henri's eyes wondered off to the trees, then to his feet, and the banked road that opened to the Rue de Venise. Yesterday, he had noted a new pain in his abdomen, and there it was again, unrelenting. Just then, he stepped into a small puddle; his ankle buckled, and he fell. He got up on one knee, clicking his tongue and wagging his head.

"Close," he muttered.

Nicolas reached over and took his arm. "Are you okay?"

Henri took a breath, pausing in the street, stood up and tested his ankle. The others behind them stopped, circled, whispering, leaning in.

"What happened?"

"Did you trip?"

"Your ankle?"

Everyone quieted. He smiled and shook his head. "I'm fine."

"My brothers," Henri looked at Nicolas first, and then around the circle. "Tell me . . . how are *you* doing?"

"I'm still hungry," Nicolas said, shook his head slowly, just twice. No one else spoke, and they walked in silence a few more paces. A hard biscuit, broth for supper. "What's going on?"

Brother Joseph[39] heard them talking, his own stomach tumbling on this evening's walk. He'd been wondering about things, noticed a change in the community, a few weeks ago. Something was not right.

"Have you seen the look on Monsieur de La Salle?" he said. "I'm telling you; something has changed . . . what about those new schools?"

They carried the worry through the neighborhood, retreating to their solicitous silence; Henri returned to his small black book, reading as he walked. The others, in different strides, did the same.

The next afternoon, after another supper of broth, bread, a bit of hard cheese with tea, the Brothers came to their recreation in the garden,

---

[39] Brother Joseph Paris joined the community over the summer, one of the new members. He was elderly man. See Loes, Augustine, FSC. *The First De La Salle Brothers 1681 – 1719*. Landover, MD: Lasallian Publications, 1999.

some sat, others walked the grounds. Monsieur De La Salle sat alone. A few Brothers started whispering together, looking over at De La Salle. It was Joseph who spoke up first, and then others joined.

"Monsieur, we can't buy what we need for our lessons."

"You are often gone to the other schools."

"Those new schools, Monsieur, four since March. We're worried."

De La Salle leaned forward. "Brothers, do you insist on dictating limits to God's Providence?"

It was Henri who spoke this time, lifted his head. "Monsieur . . . that's easy . . . ehm . . . for you to say."

Henri saw a flare in De La Salle's face. "Pardon . . . Frère Henri?"

"Now, Monsieur," Henri faltered, aware that he tapped on a boundary, but went on. "You hold an honorable station, you want for nothing . . ."

At this, De La Salle sat back, his face set. "Go on."

"This shields you, should a school close." He looked at his fellow teachers.

De La Salle crossed his arms, moved in his seat to relieve pressure from his sore leg. He flashed to the snowbank . . . *this is what I get?*

Nicolas spoke. "Monsieur . . ."

De La Salle held his gaze on Henri, turned slowly to Nicolas. "You have something . . .?

"You say . . ." Nicolas halted, then – using his left hand – tapped his chest, "that *we* ought to have faith in God's Providence." He looked at his Brothers, their coarse cloaks, recalling the day's meager meal. "If the schools close," Nicolas said, "and *they might* . . . what will happen to us?" He tapped his chest again, then pointed at De La Salle. "And what will happen to you?"

Henri joined in. "You tell us . . . we're the ones who should trust in God's Providence. We think, maybe . . . you should, too."

This confrontation follows accounts preserved in the earliest biographies of De La Salle and is referenced by De La Salle himself in his "Memoir of the Beginnings."

Over the following weeks, De La Salle traveled to Paris to meet his mentor, Père Nicolas Barré, and then with Jacques Callou, his new spiritual advisor in the wake of Nicolas Roland's death. Barré said, give up your possessions, including the canonry; and Callou told him to keep his canonry.

By the following August, De La Salle resigned his canonry and its income. He made what De La Salle biographer Bernard Hours called a "definitive break with his family" and, from then on, would live exclusively in a community with his Brothers.

Feb 22 – 25, 2011

1 message   Mon, Feb 21, 2011 at 8:53 PM

"You are God's coworkers in His work; the souls of the children you teach are the field which He cultivates through your works."

St. John Baptist de La Salle
Meditations for the Time of Retreat, 13.1

It can sometimes be hard to remember when grading a math quiz, or remonstrating with a student on the steps, or asking a worker to cinch up a tie, or trying to figure out how our grading program lost still another column of grades, that this work we do, as De La Salle claimed three centuries ago, is really about the salvation of souls.

We are here as ministers, part of salvific history, God's reach into the lives entrusted to us. The moment our students come in the front door, bequeathed to us in this small timeframe, we are for them the face *The moment our students come in the door . . . we are for them the face and fact of God.* and fact of God's presence. Probably they don't see it that way, and it's perfectly okay that they don't. However, it's vital that we do, as that faith guides what we say and what we do.

Feb 21 – 24, 2012

1 message   Mon, Feb 20, 2012 at 8:51 PM

"You must pray not only for yourself but also for those whom you are guiding."

St. John Baptist de La Salle
Meditations 187.2

We're deep into the wet and damp of a Willamette Valley winter and a couple of days away from Ash Wednesday. All around are reminders that spring is still quite a way off: leafless trees, gray skies, and Friday fasts. But we can see light at the edges of our day . . . coming to school and leaving for home, there's light, if only briefly. Our emergence from winter passes through Lent, our time of reflection.

Have I lived and worked as I have said I would?

Ash Wednesday is a blunt and sooty remembrance of our mortality. For me, Ash Wednesday helps me recall that I am bound in time, one day after another, a single life lived a certain way. As yours is. We all intersect here at De La Salle North Catholic with our students, some of whom struggle every day. But we guide them, nonetheless.

Feb 11 – 15, 2013

1 message   Sun Feb 10, 2013 at 8:17 PM

"Accept with much patience the difficulties you have to suffer."

St. John Baptist de La Salle
Meditations for the Time of Retreat, 9.1

De La Salle must've had February in mind when he wrote that line.

Okay, that was glib. To be serious, read on in the Meditation, where De La Salle notes that his young Brothers—and we, by extension—should "act with love, with sincere and true zeal . . .[be] willing to be dishonored . . . and mistreated." It's a tall order. Really, who wants to be mistreated? De La Salle instructed his young Brothers to act as if they were Christ himself, to bear the burden of the work—provide a human (practical, in this world) and Christian (salvific, for the student's soul) education for the poor, without regard to who can pay.

In a way, one might be able to take up this "acceptance" meditatively, say, in church or in a quiescent and solitary moment during a day. In the pulsed, time-stamped hubbub of De La Salle North Catholic, "difficulties [we] have to suffer" play out all the time. Every moment of every day, we face and embrace the students entrusted to us. Of course, it is not all raised hands and completed homework. Our ministry is to take on a child's anguish, to forgive a transgression, to assuage a pain, to bear a grief, so that he or she might thrive.

February drips along, day after cold, drizzly day. Our students have come off a hard push to final exams. In the linear, year-long graph of student effort, February is a trough. Knowing this may goad us to embrace our students to help them mitigate the expected lapse, keep them from falling. Be tuned to their effort, then gently lift and exhort.

123

Feb 25 – Mar 1, 2013

1 message   Sun, Feb 24, 2013 at 9:00 PM

"Have you neglected some students because they were slowest, and perhaps also the poorest? Have you shown favoritism toward other students because they were rich, or pleasant, or naturally possessing more lovable qualities than the others?"

St. John Baptist de La Salle
Meditations for Time of Retreat, 14.1

I fall sway to my natural inclinations. To the student who smiles at me, I smile in return. To the student who glowers at me, I stand rebuffed and agitated. To the pleasing and responsive student, I engage and challenge. To the recalcitrant or obtuse, I shade my words. In so doing, I am that lesser principal/counselor/teacher that De La Salle exhorts in his meditative queries: what account will you give of your instruction to those entrusted to you?

Of course, I know that my vocation is acutely understood in those least enviable moments, my shortcomings so humanly on display. In classrooms, hallways and offices every day reside the moments that quicken my heart—who will I be to the most broken and weak students among us? How will I hear the angry student? How will I reach the frustrated, low-skill reader? How will I open myself for a student's second chance? There's not an easy way in any of it . . . for these students' personal lives have so affected them that their countenance, words, or actions may repel the very person who might help them. Sometimes, I believe, we may have to take the first hit, drawing the strength to do so from our Gospel call to love, and then do what we can. It does not always work out as we hope, but our lean ought always to be for the child.

Feb 17 – 20, 2015

1 message   Mon, Feb 16, 2015 at 9:34 PM

"The zeal you are obliged to have in your ministry must be so active and so alive for your students . . . that you want to work for the salvation of their souls."

St. John Baptist de La Salle
Meditations for the Time of Retreat, 9.3

In the 1730 edition of the *Meditations* (11 years after De La Salle's death), the Foreword notes that Monsieur De La Salle composed the work because he wanted the Brothers to "appreciate the greatness of their profession as teachers and the necessity of fulfilling so holy a ministry with great fidelity to all its responsibility." There was no responsibility so great to De La Salle as the salvation of souls, an idea that may clang a bit on the rim of contemporary spirituality. For De La Salle, the young Brother before his students was as Jesus to his disciples . . . a lofty, perhaps impossible analogue, but nonetheless the model that the Founder had for all his teachers for instructing young people was then—and is now—a "holy ministry."

In the Lasallian tradition, we recognize that each adult in our school plays a role in the "holy ministry," that each child's life draws itself to God, even though that child's life

Our faith in God and each other helps us hear and see each student

may be very far from God. Our daily presence, our daily persistence—what De La Salle called "zeal"—flows out of this "holy ministry" and touches each child's heart. In this holy work, we are united for each student; our faith in God and each other helps us hear and see each student, "a letter which Jesus dictates to us and which we write in their hearts" (3rd Meditation). In this way, our zeal is a conduit of mystery that brings each child to God . . . and to their salvation.

This week, Lent's gate swings open, drawing us into a period of self-denial, a means of rendering our frenetic living into a distilled purpose. Saying "no" to something helps us recall why we say "yes" to what matters. Come Wednesday, the ashes smeared into a cross on our forehead is one such bow to a limit and, therefore, to what matters. For this Lent, let's each week place a child who may be far from God into our prayers and into our daily work.

With zeal and faith, let's love our students.

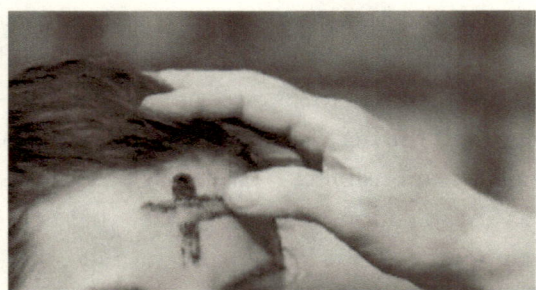

Imposition of ashes on Ash Wednesday[40]

---

[40] https://i0.wp.com/catholicpreaching.com/wp/wp-content/uploads/2024/02/ash-wednesday.jpg?ssl=1

Feb 1 – 5, 2016

1 message   Sun, Jan 31, 2016 at 8:46 PM

"Be patient toward all that is unsolved in your heart . . . try to love the questions themselves."

Rainer Marie Rilke
Letters To A Young Poet

I've always found the Second Semester of a school year filled with challenges that simply do not show up in the First Semester. There is not the effusive energy of September, but rather the stern realization that some hopes may go unmet. Instead of the bright prospect of nine fetching months to instruct and inspire, there are now four and a half months only, even though we may stare into an instructional plan that yearns for six. Rather than a focus on the full now of classroom instruction, everyone starts to pitch forward a bit into the next year . . . we do the work of this year while we simultaneously lay plans and make decisions about the next.

Rilke's advice to a young poet may just as well be advice to the young teacher, or advice to us whose mission field is a school wrestling with coming of age. One may look into a spray of work ahead—instruction, fund-raising, long-term curriculum planning, securing Work Study contracts for '16-'17, counseling students to be their best selves—and see only a wide sea of questions. Our faith in Providence's long push, and our faith in each other to match, collectively, the strain of that push with the power of our convictions . . . well, isn't that why we come here every day? We do embrace the sea of questions, loving them even, since it's the questions that call out our communal good.

⊕   ⊕   ⊕

Feb 8 – 12, 2016

1 message   Sun, Feb 7, 2016 at 8:47 PM

"You carry out a work that requires you to touch hearts, but this you cannot do except by the Spirit of God."

St. John Baptist de La Salle
Meditation 43.3, Pentecost Sunday

Today's gospel[41] talks about Jesus' walk-on preaching near the Lake of Gennesaret. A day of frustrated fishing brought Simon and his crew back to the shore, where they were washing nets. They'd caught nothing. One might guess the things they were saying. Jesus walked by them, stepped aboard Simon's boat, and started preaching to the gathered crowd. Imagine Simon . . . "Dude, what gives?"

They'd fished all morning and into the afternoon. Nada. This stranger on his boat preaches for a while and then asks them to put out to the deeper water. Simon and his crew had tossed and re-tossed nets all the live long day . . . they were a sorry, sweaty, smelly mess of weary fishermen. Poor, petulant Simon. "Um, dude . . . there's nuthin' there."

All this I can well imagine, but what follows in the Gospel narrative defies understanding. Human experience and the historical critical method can only take one so far with exegesis and, then, well . . . the nets were full, and the boats were so weighed down with fish, they feared swamping. Simon again, "Dude . . . what the . . . um, Master . . . huh?"

I've thought a lot about Simon's fatigued, disgruntled crew, cleaning nets after a long day with no fish to show for it, about Simon probably going off on Jesus. Sounds like teaching and counseling and coaching, as we witness students failing or families collapsing or teams coming apart.

---

[41] Lk 5:1-11

Maybe it sounds like mid-year at De La Salle North Catholic. The body wants a rest, to call it a day, go home . . . you know, maybe next year. And then there's this guy telling us to put out to deep water.

In some way, wherever we look about us, there is plenty of deep water. Have we faith to pull ourselves up and cast our nets out there?

As Ash Wednesday nears, Lent opens, a penitential time amid the Year of Mercy. With the Spirit of God, let's continue our work.

Blessings to you all for a holy, full-net kind of week.

Feb 13 – 17, 2017

1 message   Sun, Feb 13, 2017 at 9:19 PM

"Nothing is more significant to what makes us Catholic than the sacramental principle . . . that God is present to humankind, and we respond to God's grace through the ordinary and every day of life in the world."

Thomas Groome
What Makes Us Catholic (2002)

Jesus said, "The Kingdom of God is within you." De La Salle said he saw "all things through the eyes of faith."

Each act reveres our work with students and each other. However we imagine the Kingdom of God, the only way to it is "through the ordinary and every day of life in the world." Making phone calls, talking with students, reading papers and reports, correcting students, communicating clearly with each other, facing our inherent biases, enjoying each other in a volleyball match against students, balancing our budget, praying for and supporting each other when grief enters our lives, and the many thousands of things we do each day. Each act reveres our work with students and each other. Over time, we experience a lasting imprint of compassion and love—the hearts hold the story.

Last Thursday afternoon, I sat around a table in LYM[42] with new staff who looked back "through the ordinary and every day of life" of their first year at De La Salle North Catholic.

- They shared their collective experiences—*so varied*—of Lasallian association, what Br. Gerard Rummery, FSC, called an "essential

---

[42] Lasallian Youth Ministry Office.

130

'spirit of community' that is enshrined in Lasallian heritage." It is never one person or a subset of us, but the whole community-- *together and by association*—that teaches.

- They spoke about caring for "those most in need," that strongest strand of Lasallian education, a call to social justice through direct service of the poor. We are drawn to give special attention to those whose difficulties are most acute.

- Finally, they spoke about "Holy Ground," that we are "alert to the more in the midst of the ordinary." Do we not see this every moment we step in our school, walk amid our students, stand alongside a colleague, listen to a child's claim or lament?

This sacramental consciousness has to do with what we deem holy, that each moment is transcendent, lasts outside of itself, carried by us and our students through their day and year and out through their lives. This you do every day. That is why there is no ordinary day at De La Salle North Catholic.

Bless you all for the beauty and hope you bring to the students confided to our care.

Feb 4 – 8, 2019

1 message   Sun, Feb 3, 2019 at 8:35 PM

"An' I got thinkin', on'y it wasn't thinkin', it was deeper down than thinkin'. I got thinkin' how we was holy when we was one thing, an' mankin' was holy when it was one thing. An' it on'y got unholy when one mis'able little fella got the bit in his teeth an' run off his own way kickin' an' draggin' and' fightin'. Fella like that bust the holiness. But when they're all workin' together, not one fella for another fella, but one fella kind of harnessed to the whole shebang—that's right, that's holy."

The Preacher, on the eve of the Joad family exodus to California
John Steinbeck, *The Grapes of Wrath*, 1939

The Joad family's epic journey out of the collapsing Midwest captures a universal narrative of people in the crosshairs of natural systems that can't sustain them and human systems that exploit them. The Joad's— and all those who "are on the move"—lean into each other against these vast forces and rediscover their group strength, their capacity to keep going.

In the Lasallian narrative, De La Salle wrote to his young Brothers re- minding them that "community is a precious gem, which is why Our Lord recommended it to his disciples before he died. If we love this, we love everything. Preserve it with care, therefore, if you want your com- munity to survive."

Communities rattle and hum every day, a tumble of personal and shared storylines. Take a moment now to reflect on this intersection of your own personal life and our communal Lasallian life.

When we're "all workin' together," we create a holy force. In this way, we are strong for our students' and families.

Feb 10 – 14, 2020
1 message   Sun, Feb 9, 2020 at 8:49 PM

"Earth is crammed with heaven,
And every common bush afire with God."

Elizabeth Barrett Browning
Aurora Leigh, 1856

As a child in a Catholic school, I learned about the sacraments, imagining those seven rites as the only points of grace one could encounter. Not until my adult life did my understanding of a *sacramental consciousness* change that narrow notion from grade school. This sacramental consciousness sees the human experience as imbued with grace, if one sees it with the eyes of faith and acts with mercy and hope.

Romantic poet William Blake spoke about seeing "heaven in a wild-flower," and holding "eternity in the palm of your hand." Above, Browning summons the Old Testament story of Moses and the burning bush, God shockingly manifest in the everyday, the commonplace. The poets speak a language we translate easily . . . here at De La Salle North Catholic, we inhabit this sacramental life wherein every student and every colleague—seen with the eyes of faith—is "afire with God."

In the last two or three weeks, staff have met with students and families about grades and attendance. Each one of these moments conjures Blake, Browning, and De La Salle . . . we are always in the Holy Presence of God, and most acutely when we are with students at the edge, "those far from salvation," as De La Salle was wont to say. Those conversations are the hardest, can be the most aggravating, the most upsetting, but are *in every way* the source and substance of why this school matters.

De La Salle North Catholic is crammed with heaven . . . and every student afire with God.

It's just that, sometimes, they don't know it. Our call, our sacred work, is to remind them.

Embrace the week and the beautiful work ahead.

⊕   ⊕   ⊕

Jan 30 – Feb 3, 2023
1 message   Sun, Jan 29, 2023 at 8:27 PM

On January 7, 2023, Tyre Nichols was stopped for reckless driving by five Memphis police officers who initially pepper-sprayed and tased him; later, they kicked, punched, and beat him. Admitted to the hospital in critical condition, Nichols died three days later.

Two weeks later, January 21, in Los Angeles, a mass shooting left 11 people dead, all party-goers at a night club hosting a celebration of the Lunar New Year. It is the deadliest mass shooting in the history of Los Angeles County.

Five days later, January 26, a De La Salle North Catholic alumnus was killed near his home. He was a member of the Class of 2021.

"My God, my God, why have you forsaken me?
Why are you so far from helping me, from the words of my groaning?"

Psalm 22:1

Well, it's National Catholic Schools Week, and I am trying to get there.

In the weeks leading up to this, the anguished realities of our world keep coming, some right to our very door: the unrelenting horrors of Tyre Nichols's beating, the mass shootings in Los Angeles's Asian American community as the Lunar New Year opened, and the murder of a De La Salle North Catholic alum early Thursday morning a few blocks from his home.

Whereto?

Sorrow and grief call to the deep reservoir of fellowship and love in the people around us; a community to go to not so that one is unburdened of anguish, but so that one's anguish is heard.

One way or another, all of life's joys and all of life's losses seep into a school through the veins and hearts of all who call it home. Of course. The real world is not "out there, after high school" . . . it's right here, right now.

Even when sorrow comes to my house to spend a day with me, taps my shoulder as I lie down for a nap, or whispers in my ear as I peel potatoes . . . tomorrow, I will go to my Catholic school because of the people there, who *in faith and zeal* push on with the sacred work.

Let's be about the holy work of our school.

© Fabrice Florin/Flickr

Reflecting on February's Lasallian Meme

> "Accept with much patience the difficulties you have to suffer."
>
> St. John Baptist de La Salle
> *Meditations for the Time of Retreat, 9.1*

The Brothers line up against De La Salle. They're worried about their future. They're working as hard as they can, vigilant to their faith and their zeal; but still difficulties abide . . . and so too, therefore, does resentment toward De La Salle and the fortune and safety his personal wealth provides.

Choose a prompt to write about

➢ Write about a mounting difficulty occurring within your work. Describe the specifics of the difficulty, its resistance to be resolved, even to the point of worsening the harder you try. Patience is a gift that helps you consider deeply what is happening. How do you redress a hardship which threatens your school community?

➢ Consider a theme emerging for you this sixth month; then, write about it through this Lasallian meme of acceptance and patience, that the challenge you or your team face is telling you something deep about your work.

March

all the affection of your heart

March

"Fulfill your ministry with all the affection of your heart."

St. John Baptist de La Salle – *Meditations for the Time of Retreat, 9.1*

We are tired in March, exhausted and thinned out psychically from winter's cold and extended night times . . . empty. We count the errors and omissions of our work more than we count our successes.

What started out in September as confident teaching tumbles into fraught moments when everything takes just a little bit more than we can offer. We count the weeks to Spring Break. Then days. Then class periods.

In this seventh visitation, De La Salle leaves Reims for Paris, a three-day walk. He is 39 years old . . . and everywhere there's trouble, crises in Reims and Paris, hostile legal battles with Writing Masters, the new pastor at Saint Sulpice angles for authority over De La Salle, scurrilous accusations against De La Salle create scandal, and the Brothers' ranks thin out month by month.

How do we weather the bleak times when we feel alone in the work?

There's always a moment (or two) in a school year when the all-of-it overwhelms, when the mission seems fragile. We need, then, to lean into each other's strength and creativity; and, with all the strength of heart we can muster, press on.

⊕   ⊕   ⊕

Rue Princesse
Paris, January 1691

December, 1690, De La Salle left Paris to visit Brothers' communities in Reims. Soon after he arrived, word came from Paris that Br. Henri L'Heureux, De La Salle's handpicked successor, had himself fallen ill and the outlook was bleak. In January, De La Salle set out for Paris.

We pick him up three days out from Reims, on foot and on the road to Paris.

Water ran from Frère De La Salle's hat and cloak. Over the last few miles, his mind was wound tight with the worries back in Reims. The schools were full, and the load was heavy; exhaustion and disillusion has taken a toll; Brothers complained about their new director. Just two years ago, the Brother's community numbered 16, now it was eight. Not a single novice joined the novitiate during that time. De La Salle was not sure what to do.

This trip took longer than he expected; already, it was hours past sunset. De La Salle looked up from the road and saw the thin dome of light signaling Paris. All the troubles of this city crashed upon his imagination—the Writing Masters' legal assaults, Fr. Baudrand[43] asserting authority over him, scandalous accusations about his financial dealings, and his own long illness from which even now he felt the vestigial aches. Most of all, Brother Henri filled his thoughts. For years he was a trusted colleague with an agile mind, a faithful Brother, and now his health failing. Wherever De La Salle looked, it was all trouble and loss.

De La Salle remembered when young Henri, barely 20, was among the first to join the house on rue Sainte Marguerite. So dedicated and devote, he remained faithful even as others left. He was steady through the famines, his piety and zeal uncommon among the growing society.

---

[43] Fr. Henri Baudrand was the pastor of St. Sulpice. Though he had originally invited De La Salle to open a school in his parish, he eventually sought ecclesial authority over De La Salle and threatened the Brothers independence.

He quickly proved to be a master teacher, and De La Salle put him in charge of the young men attending the new Training College.

De La Salle entered the heart of the city and crossed the Pont Notre-Dame, the Seine below him; he saw the quivering lights from the gas lanterns over the Grand Promenade to the north. Just a block south, the towers of Notre-Dame, a dour grey façade, loomed above him, capped by the low clouds. The rain picked up. He splashed through puddles and sidestepped garbage. *At least it's cobbles and not mud.*

Across the Seine and into the narrow streets, the sewers assailed him, and a spasm seized his stomach. He recalled the complaints of the novices and Brothers . . . *we're always inside, classrooms, the chapel, the refectory, our cells* . . . the cold, cramped building, the austerity of the quarters and meals, the recurring mortifications, and the Writing Masters, the accusations of Fr. Baudrand . . . each remembrance a coiled serpent . . . the whole enterprise and the Society that served it was under threat.

He was close to Rue Princesse. His head hurt. Water dripped from his nose. With each step on the cobbles, he felt muscle tremors at his hip.

What he wanted was to dry himself and sip hot tea, say matins and retire for the night. He looked forward to visiting Br. Henri in the morning.

Streets narrowed. Rainwater sloshed off rooftops. A dog splashed by.

Finally, he was at the main door of the Brothers House and banged the knocker three times. He looked up to see a single light flaring in a room. He shivered and water flew off his coat. A few seconds later, a light glowed beneath the broad double doors. He heard the bolt withdraw and one door slowly pulled inside the vestibule where Brother Thomas[44] held a torch.

---

[44] Brother Thomas entered the community as a serving Brother in 1690. Serving Brothers wore brown cloaks, cleaned the community house, cooked the meals, and ran errands for the teaching Brothers.

"Oh . . . Monsieur . . ."

De La Salle saw the surprise in his face. "*Bonne soirée*, my dear Brother," De La Salle said, stepping through the door, removing his hat and shaking off the water. "God bless you."

Brother Thomas stepped aside to let him through.

"Monsieur de La Salle . . . *pardon* . . . we expected you sooner." He closed the door and threw the bolt closed. When he turned to De La Salle, he composed himself, moved the torch to his other hand, chewing his lower lip. "Ehm . . . Monsieur . . . Brother Henri died two days ago, God rest his soul . . . we buried him yesterday."

The academic year of 1690-1691 was fraught with personal illnesses, legal difficulties, defections of Brothers, scandalous accusations, and overreach from the Church. Nevertheless, it was the death of his heir apparent Brother Henri L'Heureux that broke De La Salle, who according to his biographer, "never . . . had his heart been dealt such a heavy blow."[45]

De La Salle secluded himself for prayer and sought advice. That summer he rented an "enclosed property with a garden" near Vaugirard, amid farmland and trees, a place for Brothers to retreat. Over the course of about 45 days, from early October and into November 1691, De La Salle rebooted the institution:

- Invited the senior Brothers to Vaugirard for a retreat that thereafter became an annual affair for all Brothers
- Began one-on-one conversations and monthly letter writing with each of the Brothers that continues to this day
- Selected Nicolas Vuyard and Gabriel Drolin to join him in professing a secret vow of "association and union," what we now know as the Heroic Vow.

---

[45] Aroz, Leon, FSC, Yves Poutet, FSC, and Jean Pungier, FSC. *Beginnings: De La Salle and his Brothers*. Romeoville, Illinois: Christian Brothers Conference, 1980.

Feb 28 – Mar 4, 2011

1 message   Sun, Feb 27, 2011 at 7:51 PM

"Fulfill your ministry with all the affection of your heart."

St. John Baptist de La Salle
Meditations for the Time of Retreat, 9.1

There are moments in our teaching and working with students when time is stripped away, just the present moment with a student. The teacher and student share a pulse—multiplying binomials, understanding the difference between Jurassic and Triassic Ages, remembering a humorous moment, correcting a poor behavior, coming to terms with a botched assignment. In this, students lean in on us, seek some health and affection perhaps not present elsewhere in their lives.

And, so, we speak to our students in a way that reminds them, we love you, especially those most trying to us. How easy to forget this or believe it not primary to our work. De La Salle's words stir us . . . we do this work with "all the affection of our hearts."

Mar 2 – 6, 2015

1 message   Sun, Mar 1, 2015 at 9:59 PM

"St. Paul says that God has a field which He cultivates, a building which He is constructing, that He has chosen you to help in this work by announcing to children the gospel of His Son and the truths that are contained in it."

St. John Baptist de La Salle
Meditations for the Time of Retreat, 1.3

The First Meditation is called "God in His Providence Has Established the Christian Schools." It was De La Salle's premise that the schools were God's mission, and he often reminded his Brothers about their young students: "appeal to them as if God were appealing through you." De La Salle understood that the work of his Christian Schools was to reach out to those students who were "far from salvation" and that the Brothers were called—*entrusted*—by God to "reconcile the young to Him." When De La Salle speaks of the "salvation of souls," he means this. Time and again, De La Salle appealed to his Brothers, at times remonstrating with them, to nurture a zeal for students far from salvation.

The more faith-filled and committed the community, the more able is the school to do the work.

Mar 29 – April 1, 2016
1 message   Mon, Mar 28, 2016 at 8:02 PM

"Remembering that God is with you will help and inspire you in all that you do."

St. John Baptist de La Salle
Letter #2, to a Brother, 15 May 1701

The noise of a school is deafening, can override meaning and purpose with seeming little effort. Put three hundred teenagers in a building, ask them to change rooms every hour, ask them to follow rules found no-where else in Portland, engage over eighty corporations, operate hundreds of computers connected to the internet . . . and the noise of it all, whether audible or metaphoric, can overrun the circuitry of one's pre-frontal cortex. The clatter-clang of now—of *Right Now!*—seems the base-line of our interconnected, time-stamped age.

In Paul Elie's *The Life You Save May Be Your Own,* he recounts the lives of four great Catholic artists of the 20th century: Thomas Merton, Walker Percy, Flannery O'Connor, and Dorothy Day. Today, I've been thinking about Dorothy Day, founder of the Catholic Worker movement who took on the system from the inside. She lived hard, flung herself at life. In her youth, she was part of the Greenwich Village's so-called "Lost Generation" and partied with Eugene O'Neill at the Hell Hole. Amid that full throttle living, she responded to something gnawing at her—the Church was moving away from the poor. It was 100 years ago, but the world she saw did not match the world she supposed. So, she took it on.

She wrote about her recurring need to step back from the noise and pres-sures of her work: remember Jesus' ministry to the poor, remember the call, remember God's presence.

146

Mar 20 – 26, 2017

1 message   Sun, Mar 19, 2017 at 8:26 PM

January brought two snowstorms separated by a few days. The first was followed by freezing rain; the second lasted two days and dropped 15" in North
Portland. It was the most snow in Portland since the 1990's.

"It is much easier for children to fall over some precipice, because they
are weak in mind as well as body, and have little understanding of what
is for their own good. They need the light of watchful guides to lead
them."

St. John Baptist de La Salle
Meditations for the Time of Retreat, 5.3

The days leading up to Spring Break are gut-check days.

This should be no surprise to anyone . . . just, if you dare, look back
through your mind's eye into the days since early January, back to school
after Christmas break. Six school-day closures followed, semester exams
pushed back a week, squeezing Term Four. Illnesses swept through the
school, a hacking cough bubbled up, it seemed, in everyone around us.
Since October 1, there have been only seven days we'd call "sunny." Me-
teorologists have declared this winter the coldest in 20 years. While an
average water year (Oct 1 – Sep 30) yields 39 inches of rain, this 2017
water year has currently poured down 45 inches . . . with over six months
to go. And have you looked at a ten-day forecast recently?

Last week, there were multiple suspensions with the SO and JR cohorts.
There are students struggling with academics, classroom comportment,
family, or drug-related issues. And so, it has been, lo, these 16 years.

Layer your professional experience over whatever your personal experience has been these last ten weeks . . . and, well, even our level-headed,

147

in-the-eyes-of-faith St. La Salle might have been reading and re-reading every scriptural passage he could find on zeal.

And yet . . . that was sun and blue-sky we witnessed yesterday. This, too, we have seen . . . students brightly breaking through to understanding or insight or gratitude.

This week let's hold each other up, shore each other up. In a new Lasallian community tradition, everyone—staff and students—will eat lunch together in the cafeteria. A chance to honor the ceaseless why of our work . . . fortified within our precious community, we each are  "watchful guides" for the beautiful students confided to our care.

You are all doing stunningly difficult work . . . out of a deep love for our students . . . and for each other.

Mar 11 – 16, 2019
1 message   Sun, Mar 10, 2019 at 8:25 PM

"By listening you minister to me."

Mr. Rogers

Watching young people listen to each other is one of the many gifts that come our way. Of course, we see this almost every day; but it is often overwhelmed by so many other instances of not listening that such moments are easy to miss.

Listening needs cultivation.

This is why our Akwantu[46] retreat is a powerful moment for our juniors. Over a few days, young men and women start to understand this: how being heard transforms their isolation. Two boys I did not know well—and who on the second day still answered most questions with "good" or "I like it" or "not too much"—by Thursday evening, they set their reticence aside and spoke in full sentences, paragraphs even, staking a claim for their place among the Class of 2020.

But we know how this goes, don't we? A whiff of community and love that is, in a short time, vexed by the pace and warp of our artificial day, laid out in 55-minute intervals, *Actively ensuring reflective time is a vital Lasallian ethos* themselves partitioned by standards and benchmarks. We'll not toss them out, of course. We assert their necessity. Only this . . . we are the

---

[46] *Akwantu* comes from Twi, a language in Ghana, and means "journey." So named by a Ghanaian student at our school who remembered the Akwantu festival back home. The Akwantu retreat is an adaptation on the very popular three-day Kairos format used by Catholic high schools across the country.

masters of the pace and the content, are we not? . . . and actively ensuring reflective time is a vital Lasallian ethos . . . and at our school, we do this regularly when we pray at the start of class. One of the first steps in cultivating listening is for students to practice listening to the divine within, something that we schedule seven times a day. We must honor that time as a moment for depth and stillness.

Keep Mr. Rogers' words close and do all you can to minister well to our beautiful students.

Mar 16 – 20, 2020

1 message   Sun, Mar 15, 2020 at 9:31 PM

Over the preceding months, we heard about a virus infecting citizens in Wuhan, China, then spreading elsewhere, ultimately reaching Washington State in late January. From there, spread was quick. Cases appeared in Arizona, Oregon, California, and Illinois. In early March the United States declared a national emergency; schools and businesses began shutting down throughout the country. COVID-19 changed everything.

"For the Spirit God gave us does not make us timid, but gives us power, love, and self-discipline."

2 Timothy 1:7

It had been moving slowly for over a week, as exponential shifts are early on. The signal was diffused, hard to hear, uncertain . . . and then, in a 24-hour period, the signal became clear, strong, and sweeping: our social structure was about to change. And then our adjectives failed us . . . words like *unprecedented* and *surreal* were not big enough. Not even 9/11 changed our daily lives as much they've changed since Thursday.

There will be some things we won't be able to know or change. There will be restrictions that will vex our best efforts. However, we made decisions on Thursday that helped our community move forward. Communication lifts our community—simply to see how people are, to see if there is more we can do for our students, to list the things we need to think about, to change or cancel or defer. We acted in the face of widening unknowns.

Alone, we fret. Together, we thrive.

Prayer, communal commitments, love, perseverance. De La Salle reminds us to look upon our work "with the eyes of faith" and then to "act with zeal."

Whatever is next, we go there together and do the sacred work—as best we can—for the students and families in our care.

© RDNE Stock project/Pexels

Feb 27 – Mar 3, 2023
1 message   Sun, Feb 26, 2023 at 9:05 PM

"Planting that orchard . . . reminded me, or illuminated for me, a matrix of connection, of care, that exists only in the here and now, but comes to us from the past and extends forward to the future. A rhizomatic care . . . that extends in every direction, spatially, temporally, spiritually, you name it."

Ross Gay[47]
On the hundreds of volunteers that planted an urban orchard
Inciting Joy (2022)

It's not every day that someone uses a rhizome as a metaphor.

In this particular case, Ross Gay uses "rhizomatic care" to talk, first, about what occurred when hundreds of people worked together over two years to turn an abandoned acre of land in Bloomington (he's a prof at the univer-  sity there) into a diverse, fruit-bearing orchard, free to all; and, second, the universal collective care of people that moves through time and which we all inhabit and are beneficiaries of, as well as contributors to, so that the *collective care continues beyond us.*

Like De La Salle North Catholic High School.

Gay's premise is that joy and pain are an "entanglement" . . . there's something about life's pain and struggle, such that joy is "what emerges from how we care for each other *through* those things."

---

[47] Ross Gay is a 2013 Guggenheim Fellow and 2015 National Book Award Finalist. Rhizome image: 2021 johan Kusuma/Shuttercock.

He writes about our alienation wrought from technology, more thumbing our phones than talking at the dinner table; about his father's death, how memory conjures what's precious; about how groups struggling to accomplish something pull off the improbable, like planting an orchard, or figuring out how to lift a school . . . and so I thought about us, our work, our impassioned disagreements, our bounded time into which we squeeze our varied and obstacle-ridden mission.

Our *entangled care* for our work, it's messy, uncertain, query-laden, sometimes self-serving, but most of the time there's that for-the-kids yank we all feel . . . and it's all happening in a manic, fast-then-slow, this-then-that, we'll-never-be-able-to-do-that, and look-what-we-did miracle of everything all at once and so we don't see it, that indestructible, irradicable rhizome of care that's keeping De La Salle North Catholic thriving.

I know you see it; or, at least, its by-product. You watch students go by, chat with them, listen to them, or just watch the myriad circles of teenagers tell stories, lean on each other in friendship, work, and school. Building their own "matrix of connections, of care."

There is so much to do, so very much, always and everywhere. As it was in the beginning, is now, and ever shall be. Let's pay attention to the "is now" part, and be grateful about that deep, continuous care "that extends in every direction, spatially, temporally, spiritually, you name it." Be generous in our care for each other so that at our leaving, we bequeath a school the future celebrates.

Mar 20 – 24, 2023

1 message   Sun, Mar 19, 2023 at 8:35 PM

"You are not far from the Kingdom of God."

Mark 12:34

At the Friday morning staff mass, our priest noted that we just passed the midpoint of Lent, a good time to take stock of our Lenten journey.

How have we used this time of introspection, repentance, and reconciliation?

No doubt, Lent is a countercultural disposition. Flies in the face of a consumer culture, where our "getting and spending"[48] oils the wheels that ought to bear us to a happy life. Of course, it rarely does. At De La Salle North Catholic, the hunkered down, dynamic whorl of our every-single-day pivots on each relationship within our community and requires spending our most personal resource—*our time* . . . for De La Salle exhorts us "to know and understand" the students in our care.

In the daily, churning mashup of 230 teenagers and 60+ adults, there's a go-go-go about it; and we all too easily yield to the frenetic pace of it. Are we not all racing to 3:31 PM on Friday? *There's so much to do!*

Let us remember . . . that's not why we are here. In the rush-push to get there (Friday, 3:31), we lay waste the community we all cherish.

Perhaps, though, we're closer to what we seek than we might want to admit. In the Gospel, the scribe underscores Jesus' recitation to love God and neighbor, and do so "with all your soul, with all your heart, with all your mind, with all your strength." No easy task, that. Here, then, Jesus' calming words resonate . . . we are "not far from the Kingdom of God."

Not far.

---

[48] Wordsworth, William. "The World Is Too Much With Us." *Poems*, 1807.

Our Lenten spiritual practice through these opening days of Spring and the manic runup to Spring Break . . . when our fatigue is like a dead weight at our ankles . . . is to go slow . . . *Let us remember . . . that we are in the holy presence of our students.* And each other.

Bless you all in this beautiful, tangled bank of our work.

©Standford University, DREME Program

Mar 4 – 8, 2024

1 message   Sun, Mar 3, 2024 at 8:39 PM

Part of our school's Lenten practice includes Friday morning staff masses before school. Various parish priests and a few Holy Cross priests from University of Portland preside, offering a spiritual morsel for those present. On this Lenten Friday, the Gospel reading was from Matthew 21 about tenants in the vineyard.

"Find a way to sit at a common table."

Fr. Bob Loughery, CSC
Superior of the Holy Cross Community
University of Portland

At last Friday morning's staff mass, Fr. Bob described the Gospel's message about the Kingdom of Heaven as not an after-death sort of thing, but rather a "kingdom of love" sort of thing. . . something we can make "present among us." He spoke of the divisions in our nation, in our communities, and in our own selves that make us rigid, making this kingdom of love less possible. Part of our almsgiving, he said, may be to "find a way to sit at a common table."

The idea got me to look in my mental mirror, and it's been on my mind over the weekend. *How do you think we're doing there?*

Once you start looking for it, there's evidence to the good:
- Every meeting—Department, Level, Leadership, Affinity Group, Club, team . . . every member at a common table, there to work for the benefit of our students
- Our students during passing time. I tossed my mental checklist, walked amid the scrambling. (Btw, get out there in the hallway. Loll, saunter, amble, stroll, meander.)

- o "I've been looking for you all morning!" shouted a distant student walking a stride ahead of me, going in the voice's direction. The shouter shouted again, "You're Student of the Month!" and then ran up and hugged her friend.
- Each staff breakfast on First Mondays when we can *literally* sit at a common table
- Colleagues saying "Hello" or "Good morning" to students and each other
- Every time you sit with a colleague to figure something out

This list is not to say that a common table means there's only smiles and puppy dog tails as far as the eye can see. Every decision made here bears the stamp of a metaphorical common table or at least ought to. The deal is that hard things are also sussed out at a common table; it's sitting at the table that makes the sussing out possible. Even though it may take a while . . . and you might not get all you hoped for.

In the days of a Brothers community at every school, regardless of the day's events and happenings, whether good or vexing, fulfilling or exasperating, they'd gather for prayer and a common meal. But we don't live at the school, do we? Our vowed, vocational life is somewhere else, and that's a wonderful thing. So we must find other ways to sit at that common table, whether it's an actual table or a compelling metaphor.

For this third week of Lent, as you walk among our students and colleagues while you fulfill your duties, think of this metaphorical, spiritual commonality, this act of charity, this common table. See what you see.

I'll pose the question again . . . *how do you think we're doing there?*

Bless you all for your remarkable resolve and your faith in our common ceaseless why—the students confided to our care.

158

Reflecting on March's Lasallian Meme

> "Fulfill your ministry with all the affection of your heart."
>
> St. John Baptist de La Salle
> *Meditations for the Time of Retreat, 9.1*

To De La Salle, hearing of Brother Henri's death was a "heavy blow," the proverbial last straw in a long run of setbacks that caused him to wonder if, after a dozen years of effort, it might all fall apart.

Choose a prompt to write about

> ➤ Consider a time when it seemed every action you took, every word you spoke, was somehow not enough, was wrong, made things worse, or was—in fact—your worst day. Why, then, did you return to the classroom, or your office, or to that insufferable task? What was it you did—or can do—to fulfill your ministry?
>
> ➤ Consider a theme emerging for you this seventh month; then, write about it through this Lasallian meme of fulfilling your mission, hard as it is, with "all the affection of your heart." What can you or your team do for you or each other to fortify your affection for the work?

April
be a watchful guide

April

"He has entrusted you especially with the care of their souls, which is what God had most at heart when He made you the guides and guardians of these young people."

St. John Baptist de La Salle – *Meditations for the Time of Retreat, 11.3*

It is the month of John Baptist de La Salle's birth (April 30, 1651) and death (April 7, 1719).

It is the month of Easter. It's worth remembering that Easter happens amid grief, renewal arising in the crisis. With all the life-bound questions that Mary of Magdala asks, all those doubts that Thomas carries, and knowing that our human circumstances often fetter our efforts, still we press on.

In this eighth visitation, De La Salle sits at his desk at Saint Yon, the Institute's home in Rouen. It's 1708, and he is about to turn 57. He's been writing letters to his Brothers for over 20 years providing direct, pragmatic advice to help guide their teaching and support their community. It's a side of De La Salle we rarely see or hear.

To what extent are we the teachers and guides our students need?

Being a good teacher takes some introspection. We must go deep into the work, have faith in our capacity to engage the professional details, to live through our questions and frailties. In this way, we are true to the path that makes our work both holy and beautiful.

⊕   ⊕   ⊕

Saint Yon
Rouen, Spring 1708

Circled by vexing challenges in Paris, De La Salle moved the novitiate and head of the Institute to Saint Yon in Rouen in 1706. The property encompassed over 16 acres with gardens and courtyards, a chapel, with plenty of room to house all the Brothers in the northern region for their annual retreat.

At the time of the move, De La Salle was 57, and there were 22 schools. As the society grew, De La Salle wrote letters to Brothers and Directors of communities to exhort and admonish them to live by the Institute's Rule and the dual charism of faith and zeal.

Of all the letters, few capture the pragmatic, direct advice as those De La Salle writes to Brother Robert, an impulsive young man who is nonetheless dedicated to the mission in Darnétal. On this spring morning in 1708, we see Father De La Salle sitting at his desk, poised to write him yet again.

It was a crisp spring morning in Saint Yon, clouds breaking up as a bright sunshine illuminated the courtyard still wet from overnight showers. Frère De La Salle said community mass in the chapel, broke his fast, and walked the grounds, his mind a tight fist from the latest news of Brother Robert's antics in Darnétal. De La Salle had not slept well, so haunted was he by the letter's contents . . . slapping a student, yelling at a neighbor down the street, and complaining about his Director. He'd already written to Brother Robert a handful of times about his impetuous behavior. He had to admit, as well, he was growing weary of the Brother's letters, a scribbling mess of misspellings and wretched penmanship.

He settled at his desk and reached for his quill. Dull, cracked. In his middle drawer, he rummaged for his pen knife, then scraped the quill's nub to a point. De La Salle held it up to the candle's light to assay the point. *Très bien.* He noticed that a few scrapings had collected on his fingers. He flicked them off, swept the lot of them onto the floor.

On one side of the table, there were a few letters received in recent days. He opened the one from Brother Robert and reviewed the troubles he'd been causing. De La Salle untied his sheaf of papers, took one out, and opened the ink reservoir. He stopped for a moment to watch the candle flame, then dipped his pen and began.

Mon très cher Frère, (My very dear Brother)[49]

I am not at all upset by the trouble that you think you have caused me. The only thing that concerns me is that you do not know what is good for you.[50]

He paused a moment and considered the line again. Too sharp? He thought not, since Brother Robert brought this on himself. He dipped his pen and continued.

It is imprudent to shout at the mothers and to chase after the children. You must be more prudent.[51]

De La Salle cringed as he pictured Brother Robert lashing out at parents and running after students. He shook his head, closed his eyes. What he must've looked like running down the street . . . *ridicule* . . . his habit and mantle flapping behind him.

Make sure that you are always the same in class and that you do not let yourself give in to impatience there. It is imprudent to throw the ferule at students, but it is disgraceful to slap them, especially in church.[52]

A breeze cooled his room, lifted the edge of De La Salle's paper so that he held it with his left hand and looked out the far window. He wondered if Brother Robert had the disposition necessary for the work. His mind wandered off to Brother Robert's start, then just 24, when he joined as a serving Brother, a devout, prayerful man who wanted to teach. The problem was, he couldn't seem to get out of his own way – he needed reminders to keep the primacy of class time, and to promote only those who are ready.

---

[49] De La Salle uses this phrase to open every letter he writes to a Brother. The letter in this vignette is a composite from four different letters. All references to specific letters come from *The Letters of John Baptist de La Salle*, volume 1 of Lasallian Resources: The Complete Works of John Baptist de La Salle. The Christian Brothers Conference, 1988.
[50] Letter 47: 1 [1709].
[51] Letter 39: 6 [May 1, 1708]
[52] Letter 44:15 [April 26, 1709]

We must omit some spiritual exercise rather than take class time to complete a necessary errand, for we must not lose a minute of class. Do not promote students to a lesson for which they are unprepared. Be careful about this; otherwise, they will learn nothing.[53]

Enough for now. There are more letters to write. His dipped his pen a last time and scribed a reminder about his fellow Brother at the Darnétal school and what he must not fail to do.

See to it that both of you live by the Rule and are closely united and that you are as respectful to your Brother as to people in general.[54]

I am, in our Lord, my very dear Brother,

Totally yours,[55]

De La Salle

Brother Robert went on to become the Director of the Darnétal community and remained a Christian Brother until his death in 1734.

---

[53] Letter 41:6, 9 [December 7, 1708]

[54] Letter 41:13

[55] De La Salle closed each letter to a Brother in this way.

Apr 2 – 5, 2012

1 message   Sun, Apr 1, 2012 at 8:57 PM

"To touch the hearts of your students is the greatest miracle you can perform."

St. John Baptist de La Salle
Meditation 139.3, on the Feast of St. Peter

There is likely no other quotation that distills the Lasallian vocation so well as this one. Reading De La Salle's meditations—and even his comprehensive *Conduct of the Christian Schools*—one comes to understand that a Brother's (and a Teacher's) faith in one's teaching, as a conduit of God's grace, is the source of this charism. De La Salle believed it absolute that his work and the broader work of the Brothers fulfilled a chief ministry of the church—bearing witness to God's love among the weak and poor of 17th century France. When we begin every day and every class "remembering that we are in the Holy Presence of God," let's also remember that we come to this work as ministers.

After weeks of a reflective Lent, we enter Holy Week, the annual round wherein the church recounts the core story of faith, what besets us in this mortal coil and what lies beyond. I suspect that Holy Week touches each of us differently, but there is no forestalling mortality. The narrative of Holy Thursday and Good Friday depicts our dark human frailties—betrayal, fear, isolation, physical suffering, but ultimately, a courageous submission. In these days ahead, spend some reflective time about our life and how we live it here at De La Salle North Catholic with our students who sometimes don't know what's happening around them or who can be as obstinate as Peter. It is our frailty, after all, that signals a need for miracles; it's why each of us must act in faith in our work and "touch the hearts" of our students.

166

Apr 29 – May 3, 2013

1 message   Sun, Apr 28, 2013 at 8:20 PM

"He has entrusted you especially with the care of their souls, which is what God had most at heart when He made you the guides and guardians of these young people."

St. John Baptist de La Salle
Meditations for the Time of Retreat, 11.3

Have you ever considered that you are God's tenderness manifest in the lives of the young people we serve?

This is so profound and so disquieting when one considers what such an obligation means, especially as we sometimes (or often) are called to correct the behavior of a student. De La Salle wrote quite a bit about correction—when it is to be done, how it is to be done, and why it is to be done. De La Salle speaks primarily of disposition—that is, what is in the mind and heart of the teacher or administrator so that the correction, with care, is received by the student?

On Friday, I found myself, on multiple occasions, facing a student or two and needing to correct behavior. In the vortex of those moments, I must say that the "care of their souls" was not first on my mind. Two days later, while threading weeds from what will be my tomato patch, my mind replayed through those exchanges. De La Salle's exhortation—itself a tender reminder to overcome our diffidence—arrived as both consolation and challenge. The epochal arc of providence lands us all here, at De La Salle North Catholic High School . . . in this school year . . . and with the students entrusted to us.

May we all be for our students the guides and guardians which "God had most at heart."

Apr 14 – 18, 2014
1 message   Sun, Apr 13, 2014 at 8:05 PM

"When you encounter some difficulty in the guidance of your disciples, turn to God in confidence."

St. John Baptist de La Salle
Meditations for the Time of Retreat, 4.1

All I can say about De La Salle's dictum is, "easier said than done." This time of year, there are always difficulties. And since many other times I may have "turned to God in confidence" to little effect, I grow weary of this piety. How do I keep my heart and head in the life of a difficult disciple?

Recently, a former student of mine (now 38 and not Catholic) told me, "I really like your Pope." And, well, I really do, too. In his *Evangelii Gaudium (The Joy of the Gospel)*, he asserts that faith is "inseparable from self-giving." He goes on to talk about community and reconciliation, how these graces are bound up in our faith in the improbable—Easter morning. At the end of this section, Francis concludes by stating this faith calls us "to a revolution of tenderness."

Again, there are times when tenderness is far from my thoughts. But, in De La Salle and Pope Francis are two sacred assertions exhorting we who serve to do the unlikely, to do the improbable and difficult: to have faith and be tender. Tenderness is the physical reach of an empathic heart—there's a memory there, reminding us of what *we* needed in some past pain and anguish.

In these days of a Holy Week, when our mortality seems ever more tenuous, let's partake in Francis' "revolution of tenderness" and tend to the difficulties of our students with much care and faith and love.

168

Apr 6 – 10, 2015
1 message   Sun, Apr 5, 2015 at 9:37 PM

"Wherever I go I will find you, my God."

St. John Baptist de La Salle
Explanation of the Method of Interior Prayer

The day after Jesus' death was most certainly a desolate day. Three years of a surging ministry that seemed ready to break through to change ended violently with the trial, torture and killing of Jesus. Stunned and shocked, his followers scattered and hid. Throughout the day, grief bore down on his mother, his dearest friends, his disciples. Likely, they did not eat, did not talk much, wept some; every action felt weighted down, just to speak a thought expended so much energy that they'd then lay quiet. They'd look out a window or from a rooftop to see the now empty Golgotha. It really happened. It was true. The Teacher was dead and all that was hoped for was gone. A thing of the past.

Still dark, Mary Magdalene stole out Sunday morning to anoint her friend's body. She came upon the improbable . . . the stone rolled away. She looked inside. Empty. Some folded linens. Was there panic? Was there fear? Against all previous evidence, Mary Magdalene embraced hope. The past offered her nothing; everything lay in the future.

Apr 4 – 8, 2016
1 message   Sun, Apr 3, 2016 at 8:34 PM

"Know your students individually and be able to understand them."

St. John Baptist de La Salle
Meditations, 33.1, how teachers should act toward their pupils

Most mornings, I step outside to the back stoop about 7:45 with coffee, bundled up, and greet students as their parents drop them off. Last week, it's been glorious on sunny mornings, Mt Hood poking its peak above the tree line, the sky lit up. Tri-Met buses and MAX trains deposit students at nearby stops, and—in small groups—our students walk west on Lombard to the ramp between the portables and then circle back to the cafeteria door. With the sun, the walk has been leisurely.

Students climb from cars, pull a bag or two from the floorboard or from the trunk, hoist them over a shoulder, and say good-bye to a parent or grandparent on a school drop-off run, younger children in the backseat look up at me and wiggle-wave their small hand. They carry projects and lunches, some carry breakfast. Some students emerge from a car laughing; some launch from the car before it stops, a sharp voice rising once the door opens, and a student slams the door; some students climb from a driver's seat, and I comment how much more treacherous are Portland streets with a new driver on them . . . always there's a polite laugh.

Every parent knows this moment Students see a friend and call out. *. . . leaving your child with other* Students and occasional staff *people, a moment of tender trust.* members join me there, chat a moment, and we shake the hands of arriving students. It's a threshold moment—leaving family behind, stepping through a doorway into a separate world called De La Salle North Catholic High School. Every parent knows this moment . . . leaving your

170

child with other people, a moment of tender trust. Some parents wait, let their car idle as their child climbs the stairs, shakes my hand, and steps inside. Then, and only then, do they drive off. Others make the loop-turn in the parking lot, look left from their seat to watch their child enter the building. What will her day be like? Will he be okay today? And then they drive off, out the parking lot, a right onto Russet Street toward Interstate Avenue, and then out from the neighborhood to their own day.

I wonder what narrative unfolds in each ride to school. One morning, an SUV pulled up, mom driving, grandmom in the passenger seat. A back door opened and out climbed a student who, first, walked around the car to his mom, kissed her, and then came around the front to his grandmother, who kissed her grandson and blessed him with a sign of the cross. There, right there . . . that is why people choose this school, choose to make sacrifices so their children can be here, choose to spend their day with you.

You do such good work. Every day. And our families know it, trust you, have faith in you to know and care for their precious child. Bless you and your beautiful work.

Apr 17 – 21, 2017
1 message   Sun, Apr 16, 2017 at 8:08 PM

"On the first day of the week, Mary of Magdala came to the tomb early in the morning, while it was still dark."

John 20:1

Living can seem an accumulation of losses, heaped up against, obliterating, the earliest dreamscapes of one's hoped-for life. As it is now, so must it have been even more so given what the people of Jesus' community experienced living beneath the heel of Rome, a people oppressed, ridden hard. It is not much to imagine their rallying around him, surging to him throughout Galilee.

"I have come that you might have life, life to the full," he often said. Throngs flowed toward him. And then it all seemed to unravel rapidly, leaving people bewildered, alone, fearful.

Jesus radically embraced this mortal coil, yielding to temporal power, but faithful to God, to his own divine transcendent truth. His searing submission is what lifts us to this day, *for through it,* we are made strong, made one, our gem of the De La Salle North Catholic community that is each day the face of God's divine truth for the students in our care.

Can you place yourself in Mary Magdalene's walk that morning? Bereft, but duty-bound still, her sandaled feet plodded from home; up before her friends, up before the birds, she must've wrapped herself against the cool  night air. She was alone with her disquieting thoughts: heart-broken, mind-racing, as the events of the last few days played and replayed in her head. Maybe she could have said something, could have prevailed upon Judas, warned Jesus, something to stop what was happening; the second-guessing must have been an escalating burden. Nonetheless, she was determined to anoint Jesus' body, so on she walked in the desert night air.

I wonder about Mary[56], her first raw thoughts . . . what flashed in her head when she saw that empty tomb . . . when she trembled there with only questions.

Blessings to each of you this Easter Week, this unexpected week.

---

[56] Image of Mary Magdalene from chromosometwo.wordpress.com/2016/03/04that-fuzzy-empty-tomb/

"In the light of faith, you see the world quite differently."

St. John Baptist de La Salle
Letter #118, to a laywoman

To "see the world differently" means what?

In *The Forest Unseen* (2012), biologist David Haskell narrates the interconnected life of an old growth forest in southeastern Tennessee, near the Cumberland Plateau, by visiting a one-square meter patch of the forest floor "many times a week," for one year. Haskell invokes both William Blake ("to see the World in a Grain of Sand") and St. Francis Assisi in his hermitage as he searches "for the universal within the infinitesimally small." Haskell calls his one square meter patch his "forest mandala."

So, I wondered . . . what is my one square meter at De La Salle North Catholic? What recurring experience or oft-visited place is my Lasallian mandala?

One of the vital marks of a Catholic school is what Thomas Groome (*What Makes Us Catholic*) calls the "sacramental consciousness," a capacity to "encounter the sacredness of the ordinary." Even as you read this, you are likely to light upon a memory of such a moment here at school, when the vastness and holiness of your work broke through. But let's be frank, the big moments that flash obviously before our eyes are rare . . . and they're rare because we are seldom looking. There's always a checklist that veils the liminal experience.

Teachers know this well . . . there is never enough time to get it all done . . . there is always a lesson to plan, a lab to prepare, a parent to call,

174

papers to read, a test to write, a meeting to attend, a lunch duty to fulfill, a field trip to organize, a dance to chaperone. The work is never completed. It's just that, eventually, it's June.

Our everyday can be a dead sprint with *what* after *what*, a litany of *this* and *that* and *those* and *be sure to*. However, our vitality as a Lasallian Catholic school depends on our capacity to encounter the *why* for this is how we nourish ourselves and sustain our community. This is why, seven times a day, we speak aloud, "Let us remember . . . that we are in the holy presence of God."

What is your one square meter at De La Salle North Catholic? How often do you visit there?

Blessings to us all amid our every day.

Apr 3 – 6, 2023
1 message   Sun, Apr 2, 2023 at 8:54 PM

"Let the way you live be that of the Gospel."

St. John Baptist de La Salle
Meditations, 84.3, regarding the apostle Thomas

De La Salle wrote this line in reference to Thomas's doubts, his call for evidence, which fortified an emerging faith spurring him to preach the Gospel widely. To De La Salle, the story of Thomas was a way to remind his teachers that one must live a certain way, a life with a pure heart, open to others . . . "let the way you live be that of the Gospel."

His meditation on St. Thomas is not surprising, since De La Salle's life-long memes are faith and zeal, our Lasallian inheritance.

We have times when it appears our efforts come up empty   This time of year, seven months in, we have times when it appears our efforts come up empty, our work feckless. Our human nature betrays us, fills us with doubt, and we warm ourselves in our pathos . . . where's the evidence that my work means anything? Like Thomas, unless I see proof, I will not believe.

Our spiritual practice, now an act of fatigued courage, is to live Jesus' message of the Sermon on the Mount . . . reminder after reminder of how to live with "virtues deeper than the Scribes and Pharisees" . . . to see the transcendence, the sacredness of my students.

In this way, we are true to our call, true to our faith, true to our Lasallian charism, the evidence of it being our zeal to keep going.

Many blessings of holy courage as you carry out your beautiful work.

⊕   ⊕   ⊕

Apr 2 – 5, 2024
1 message   Sun, Apr 1, 2024 at 8:37 PM

"Faith is disorderly and intermittent and full of surprises . . . faith is a stranger, an exile on the earth, and doesn't know for certain about anything. Faith is homesickness. Faith is a lump in the throat. Faith is less a position *on* than a movement *toward*—less a sure thing than a hunch. Faith is waiting. Faith is journeying through space and time."

Frederick Buechner, novelist
Spoken in a lecture series in the New York Public Library, Winter 1987[57]

I read Buechner's passage over spring break while in Depoe Bay, looking out into a stormy ocean, rain battering the windows, winds so strong it was breezy *inside* our closed door. There's a lot in Buechner's list—a stranger, an outcast, a doubter, a prodigal child, lump in the throat, more verb than noun, one who waits, finding a plot in what he later called the "higgledy-piggledy experience" of daily life. I was drawn to it because it sounded a lot like any day at De La Salle North Catholic.

I don't know if Buechner is right, only that, right now, something rings true there about my faith experience, more storyline than catechism, a ricocheting mashup of steadiness and chaos. Faith is not a monolithic thing, nor some divine AI on a mountaintop delivering all the answers. No. We're all a little bit lost, pilgrims finding our way through the everydayness of our work, illumined now and again—*there!*—something breaking through, a transcendence, the way the ceaseless continuity of the Pacific's waves tells you something about eternity.

And this has to do with De La Salle how?

---

[57] Zinsser, William, Ed. *Spiritual Quests*. Book-of-the-Month Club, Inc. New York, 1988.

I believe I've mentioned Br. Robert (1676 - 1734) before, a Brother who received all manner of reprimand in several letters from De La Salle (11 in ~18 months) because he was *always* having a hard time (yelling at neighbors, talking during community silence, walking out of classes, not purchasing class materials, his handwriting was illegible and spelling atrocious, sort of the Inspector Clouseau[58] of Christian Brothers). I bring him up again because, well, he seems a good example of an earnest human trying to do the right thing but tripping over himself. A lot. De La Salle's frank persistence with him—reminding him to be cordial and punctual, to stay in the classroom, and to see his community as a source of grace—underscores, I believe, a deep Lasallian meme. However we might understand "being saved," our daily work at De La Salle North Catholic is one of the ways it happens.

Bless you all in your beautiful, higgledy-piggledy[59] work.

---

[58] Inspector Clouseau is a bumbling and improbably successful French detective in the movie series *The Pink Panther*, played by Peter Sellers.
[59] Such a fun word, higgledy-piggledy. Etymologists think it's from a 16th century children's jingle about the chaos of herding pigs.

Apr 22 – 26, 2024
1 message   Sun, Apr 21, 2024 at 8:10 PM

I don't know exactly what a prayer is.
I do know how to pay attention,
how to fall down into the grass,
how to kneel in the grass,
how to be idle and blessed,
how to stroll through the fields,
which is what I have been doing all day.

Mary Oliver
"The Summer Day"

Do you know "how to be idle and blessed" at De La Salle North Catholic? To stroll through the school . . . to kneel amid its life and vitality?

We're closing in on the end of another school year, the last one for the Class of 2024 as they continue their series of exits from us, which started back in September when we asked them to "Stand Up and Lead."[60] And then there came October and November and December and January and February and March and, now . . . April 22, so near the end of their four-year, Lasallian corridor.

So . . . when does it begin, this exiting from childhood?

I suppose it's different for each of our Seniors, a moment that marks them, but they may not know it for what it is until some later time in their life; looking back, *yeah*, they'll say, *it started right there*. Let's pay attention . . . since it will be unfolding right in front of us . . . their last retreat,

---

[60] The Leadership Assembly was our way of calling the Seniors to be leaders and exemplars for the younger students in our school. Seniors received a hand-written note from a staff member and a St. La Salle medal.

their last St. La Salle Day, the prom, College Sweatshirt Day, their last workday, and their last day of classes, just a little over four weeks from today.

This will be new to them—that slow, accumulating realization, deeply felt, that they're not coming back, that their next thing is to exit.

To echo Oliver's sense of prayer, let's pay attention . . . since what we attend to, we make holy.

Bless you all in your beautiful work.

⊕   ⊕   ⊕

Reflecting on April's Lasallian Meme

> "He has entrusted you especially with the care of their souls, which is what God had most at heart when He made you the guides and guardians of these young people."
>
> St. John Baptist de La Salle
> *Meditations for the Time of Retreat, 11.3*

Every month since fall 1691, De La Salle wrote letters of guidance and encouragement to his Brothers. As it was with Brother Robert, De La Salle was pragmatic, specific to a needed correction, and demonstrated care of his colleague.

Choose a prompt to write about

➢ Consider a student who represents a steady challenge to you, who needs recurring correction, may even be a thorn in your side. Write about your response to that student and the "care of their soul," what it means that "you are entrusted" to your students, that no matter your role in the school you are to be a "guide and guardian."

➢ Write about a theme emerging for you this eight month; then, consider it through this Lasallian meme of believing you are what "God had most at heart." How can you or your team sustain the needed care when circumstances and your own limits vex your best hopes?

May

care and vigilance

May

"You have been called by God to this ministry, and you have been given the grace of teaching and the gift of exhortation for the sake of those entrusted to your responsibility. Use these gifts you have received with care and vigilance."

St. John Baptist de La Salle – *Meditations for the Time of Retreat, 1.2*

⊕　⊕　⊕

To care for someone starts with attention, with vigilance. In May, that's hard to do, since the closer to school's end, the harder and murkier everything seems. The ghost voices of our own doubts linger in breaks and echo in our lesson plans; we look back, winsome, through winter and fall to the late summer when the school year opened.

In this ninth visitation, we see De La Salle, now 62, emerge from the chapel at a hermitage called Parmenie. He walks the grounds and sits on a bench to look out over the Isère Valley and the snow-capped Chartreuse Mountains near Grenoble, hundreds of miles from Paris. He wonders about his 35 years of establishing schools and training teachers.

What is required of you in May?

Our students and colleagues need our presence, need our gifts to teach and exhort. This, we can only do by the vigil we keep – so, through our diligent care for each other and steady vigilance of our students, we keep teaching.

Parmenie, near Grenoble, France
March 1714

Father de La Salle left Paris for Provence in Lent, 1712. Against a backdrop of civil and ecclesial conflicts in Paris, his visit to the south of France was like a homecoming; clerics welcomed him warmly; they supported the Brothers and advocated for more schools.

One year later, the good vibes were gone. Local pastors' support for De La Salle waned, plans dried up for a new school as did financial backing for a novitiate in Marseille. In a trip to Mende[61], the Brothers' community refused him entrance. It felt like Paris all over again. At the same time, his rheumatism had been acting up.

Leaving Mende, De La Salle travelled to Grenoble where Brother Jean Jacquot, the Director of the Community, welcomed him and provided seclusion, prayer, and rest. For a time, De La Salle made himself scarce. In March 1714, he walked up to Parmenie, staying for several weeks, filling in for the hermitage's chaplain. This early Spring afternoon, we see De La Salle emerge from the chapel.

De La Salle walked out from afternoon prayer, cloak tied at his neck, hat tight on his head, buffeted from the northerlies this late March afternoon. Events and changes in the Institute seized him still. He wondered about what's next. His latest bout with rheumatism brought him to death's door a third time. Still weak from his treatment, the journey from Grenoble was slow and occasionally painful, especially from the Isère River up to the hermitage at Parmenie. But he was out of the city, away from the work. Here, he looked out from the eastern ridge. De La Salle took a deep breath, felt the jolt of chill air, held it, and exhaled. He closed his eyes and, again, another breath. It was quiet. No accusation, no ridicule, no voices at all.

"I could get used to this," he said aloud.

---

[61] In south, central France, about 200 miles west of Grenoble.

Fog layered the Isère Valley, only Parmenie and the distant Chartreuse Mountains rose above it. Up here in the high place of Parmenie— the cities obscured, he embraced solitude.

My whole life through, he thought, *I have done as I ought.* He yawned, threw his arms out to encompass the full panorama and depth of the view, as if reaching out might bring the landscape's serenity into his very body. Last night, the nightmare had returned . . . distorted faces yelling, Brothers leaving, schools shuttered, books and furniture tossed into the street, set afire . . . Reims and Paris appeared as a single rainswept rock wall as he, sopping and shoeless, rambled at the edifice, searching for an exit. It's a dark night, that dream, and it came to him frequently.

He sat on a bench there, overlooking the fogbound valley, and felt every year of his advanced age. He thought of the harvest festivals when a child in Reims, Nicolas Roland and the sisters there, that meeting with Adrien Nyel and, together, establishing new school. *I was only 28*, he mused, nodding at the absurd turns of his life. Those first Brothers . . . the house on Rue Neuve, schools in Paris, Rouen, Calais, the Provence . . . and now, nearly 80 Brothers. *What was I thinking?*

His hip hurt, another spasm. These happened regularly, no longer severe but annoying, limiting.

His mind whirled back among the early days, those improbable times, a mystifying God yanking him ahead to the next thing. He was seeing it all. *My God,* he thought, *if I had known what all this would bring.*

He calmed his mind, took a long, tedious breath and closed his eyes, tilted his head back and let the wind hit his face.

The reminiscence brought Brother Jean Jacquot to De La Salle's mind, the story playing back from 30 years ago when Jean was a boy of ten who enrolled at the Brothers school in Château-Porcien; then, at 14, he was Brother Jean, a novice when the House on Rue Neuve opened; at 22, he was among the 12 who took the first vows; he joined De La Salle in Paris when he was 27; and here in the Grenoble, suddenly, he's 42 and Director of the community.

"Whatever you need, Monsieur De La Salle," he had said. "We'll find a way."

De La Salle sat a few more minutes in that reverie of those long-ago early days figuring everything out; and now, the trials of the present times, running nearly two dozen schools located throughout the country.

He stood and walked back to his room. There was work to do.

Concerned about the state of the Society, the Brothers in Reims and Paris sent De La Salle a letter dated April 1, 1714, pleading for him to return to Paris.

We very humbly beseech you, and we command you in the name and on the part of the body of the Society to which you have vowed obedience, to take up at once the general government of our Society.

Though initially reluctant, De La Salle returned to Paris and took up the mantle of Superior of the Christian Brothers.

In fall 1718, De La Salle's health declined, his rheumatism intensified, and he suffered asthma attacks. By March, De La Salle was confined to his bed. On April 3, he drew up his will, directing the Brothers "to carry out their work with zeal and selflessness." He died on Good Friday, April 7, 1719.

At the time of his death, there were 26 communities and schools in France, one in Rome, and about 100 Christian Brothers.

May 23 – 27, 2011

1 message   Sun, May 22, 2011 at 9:04 PM

"Let it be clear . . . in all your relations with the children who are entrusted to you that you look upon yourself as ministers of God, acting with love, with a sincere and true zeal, accepting with much patience the difficulties you have to suffer, willing to be dishonored and mistreated, even to give your life for Jesus in the fulfillment of your ministry."

St. John Baptist de La Salle
Meditations for the Time of Retreat, 9.1

Granted, De La Salle was speaking to vowed Brothers in this meditation. But . . . "willing to be dishonored and mistreated . . . give your life"?

These are strong challenges—even 300 years ago—to grown men who were faced with teaching poor boys off the streets of Reims, France. I have no doubt that as we read De La Salle's words, we understand and live them out in varying degrees.

In Portland, we collectively receive young people a day, each of them bearing a wound or pain we often cannot see; we have been, at some times, dishonored or mistreated; we have suffered difficulties in this ministry. At times, it may very well seem that we are giving our life to them. Our faith in God and love for our students must be sufficiently strong to take on such struggle, to carry the responsibility providentially entrusted to us. It is for this reason that De La Salle created communities where such faith and zeal might be fostered. And, just so, we too must lean into each other a bit, hoist our colleagues, pray for strength and, well, hang on. June cometh.

⊕   ⊕   ⊕

May 20 – 24, 2013
1 message   Sun, May 19, 2013 at 8:40 PM

"Do your part to help build up the kingdom of God in the hearts of your students."

St. John Baptist de La Salle
Meditations, 67.1, on abandonment to Providence

Catholic schools separate themselves from other schools when the life of a student explodes with trouble or anguish. In such dire moments, our commitment to a mission—in our case, to provide a human and Christian education, especially to the poor—draws us close to families and students in a way other institutions cannot be. It is also the hardest, most daunting work we do, where clear answers are elusive, and results of our efforts may not be known for a long time.

In the last few weeks, recent dishar- *How do we balance* mony among some students has *the good of the students with* called us to such a moment. What *the good of the school?* does our charism call us to do for these students and their families? How do we balance the good of the students with the good of the school? What does De La Salle's directive for us to "build up the kingdom of God in the hearts of [our] students" compel us to do? There being no ready look-up answer to any of these, we lean in to our vocation with zeal: to be gentle and yet firm, to keep uppermost the good of the child (and—on this Pentecost Sunday—to invoke the gifts of the Holy Spirit to guide our sacred work.

We are 35 weeks into a 38-week school year. We feel it in our bones. In this week and those remaining, let's all "do our part"—whatever that part may be—with passion, with determination, and most of all with love.

189

May 19 – 23, 2014
1 message   Mon, May 18, 2014 at 5:38 PM

"It often happens that students do not have enough strength of body or mind to bear the burdens which many times overwhelm them."

St. John Baptist De La Salle
The Conduct of the Christian Schools

Two students—one current, one former—just last week emerged from the shadowy creases wrought by their life circumstances: a junior student in the throes of mental distress sat with our counselor and me along with her mother and haltingly told us her pressures; and a sophomore, now attending a public school, who had run away from home came by our school to thank our staff for helping her family.

In both stories, we hear the lament of so many of our students; they shoulder sharp, long-held burdens. Even our broad, compassionate instruction and intervention cannot lighten these loads sufficiently to keep them from calamity. In some cases, we call police; in rare cases, we may dismiss a student, an act seemingly antithetical to our mission. No decision is harder. Either way, we know the bottom of a student's life is a painful place, but it is sometimes a necessary moment so that a student and a family can begin to right themselves.

The quotation above comes from Chapter 5 of *The Conduct of the Christian Schools* where De La Salle writes about "Corrections," a task he describes as "one of the most important things to be done in the schools." Here, he opens the dichotomy: "act toward (students) in a manner at the same time both *gentle and firm*"(italics mine). Recognizing this obvious contradiction, he wisely frames the outer boundaries in a question: "What must be done in order that firmness may not degenerate into harshness and that gentleness may not degenerate into languor and weakness?"

190

For a moment, consider the many times in a school day we face such a paradox with our students, a few times acutely. And remember, further, that we are for them an older sister or brother or, perhaps, parent – the lone, steady adult in their lives. Here, we can only ask, what does this student need from me?

A last thought . . . when De La Salle wrote about zeal, he had May in mind. Remain beholden to Solomon-like discretion even though, nine months into this year, fatigue weakens our capacity. Whence comes zeal? Only faith.

In their hearts, they love you. Be there for them.

May 27 – 30, 2014

1 message   Sun, May 26, 2014 at 9:32 PM

"When you encounter some difficulty in the guidance of your disciples, turn to God with confidence."

St. John Baptist de La Salle
Meditations for the Time of Retreat, 4.1

This is the last week of school for The Class of 2014. And with most milestones, there's a mix of true things, emotional and psychological erratics, and the heavy sweetness of the long goodbye. The messy day-to-day of class periods and work schedules and school work and lunch on Lombard somewhere and the variance of home-life are the slow, slow beat of April into May; in these last days, our cultural norms soon take over the humdrum and scale it all up to the high ritual of a Threshold Crossing—graduation, replete with vestments, processions, Valedictory speeches, traditional music, celebrations, community and family gatherings, blessings and Commencement speeches from the elders. Slowing the threshold moment down while also dressing it up imbues the experience with the importance it well deserves. It is our milestone, too, after all.

This Tenth Commencement of De La Salle North Catholic High School is also its largest. The Class of 2014 has 74 students, five Valedictorians, three Gates Scholars, and the highest four-year retention rate (67%) since the Class of 2005 (70%). Their Math and Science ACT scores are the highest in the school's history. This is a group of students who have also excelled in athletics with teams and individuals earning State recognition. Many of our students have conducted service at our school as well as throughout their community so that honors and scholarships and other recognitions have flowed to them.

Of course, it's not all sweetness and light. Every year, we arrive at these closing days wondering if, indeed, some of our students will close the deal. The onrush of adult expectation and realizing that soon they'll be jettisoned from a known world, albeit chaotic, unleashes emotions and odd psychological turns among our soon-to-be alumni. Some will struggle right up the end to earn the necessary credit. Being students at De La Salle North Catholic, though it announces hopeful destinies, does not remove the conditions that qualified them to be here in the first place. In fact, those conditions very seldom vanish, but indeed dog them unto the hard-fought finish they seek.

Being free of De La Salle, while empowering and hopeful, can fill our seniors' days and dreams with turmoil and fear. There's terrifically hard work still to do in these remaining days. And then in the interim days running up to departing home for college. In the opening line of Charles Dickens masterful work *David Copperfield*, the novel's namesake wonders, "whether I shall turn out to be the hero of my own life." It was not until many decades later that he could rightly answer his own question. In short, there's heroic work still to come.

Days remain. Let's gather ourselves to stoke our zeal for this stretch run.

May 2 – 6, 2016
1 message   Sun, May 1, 2016 at 9:40 PM

"You have been called by God to this ministry, and you have been given the grace of teaching and the gift of exhortation for the sake of those entrusted to your responsibility. Use these gifts you have received with care and vigilance."

St. John Baptist de La Salle
Meditations for the Time of Retreat, 1.2

The coupling of our two celebrations this week is apt: Teacher Appreciation Week and Founder's Week.

John Baptist de La Salle was canonized on May 24, 1900, and declared the Patron Saint of Teachers on May 15, 1950. In his lifetime, he founded free schools for the poor; chose the vernacular over Latin as the teaching language much to the disdain of his bishops; wrote a how-to text for school operations called *The Conduct of the Christian Schools* that was a best seller in Europe for nearly 200 years; and devoted his life to the spirituality of professional teachers. It is well for us to remember that he forswore his own church career (a likely cardinal appointment) to foster a community of teachers. In short, he broke from clergy and chose the path of laity.

And this has been the hallmark of Lasallian schools around the globe – in relationship with our students, we bear witness to our faith. De La Salle North Catholic High School is a Catholic school because of its sponsorship by the De La Salle Christian Brothers and operates in Portland at the invitation of the Archdiocese. All true. However, as a Lasallian school, we respond to a broad community need to provide, as mentioned last week, "a human and Christian education, especially the poor," irrespective of our students' religious affiliations.

Did you know there are Lasallian schools without a single Catholic student in them? Did you know that Bethlehem University[62], about 80% Muslim, is run by the Christian Brothers? Did you know that there are two public charter high schools[63] in Chicago run by the Christian Brothers? What's up with these guys?

What's up with these guys is not too different from what was up with them 330 years ago when De La Salle gathered his first teachers in Reims, France. Teach students what they need to learn for a practical life, form them morally, and hold your community as dear as family . . . Brothers to each other and older Brothers to your students.

This first week of May, we honor our Lasallian heritage celebrating our extraordinary instructional team who every day touch hearts, teach the long virtues of mental courage and habits of mind that sustain livelihoods and communities for decades to come.

Thank you for your profound ministry to the students in our care.

---

[62] As of Fall 2024, the Muslim student population of Bethlehem University was 82%.
[63] Arne Duncan, then Superintendent of Chicago Public Schools, asked the Christian Brothers to open two public charter schools. As of Summer 2025, those two public charter schools—Catalyst Maria and Catalyst Circle Rock—continue with established Lasallian traditions.

May 23 – 27, 2016

1 message   Sun, May 22, 2016 at 6:41 PM

"Your zeal for the children you instruct would not go far and would not have much result or success if it limited itself only to words. To make it effective it is necessary that your example support your instructions, and this is one of the main signs of zeal."

St. John Baptist de La Salle
Meditations for the Time of Retreat, 10.3

Every seasonal boundary shows itself adjusting, like the one we're in, with some wild swings from a dry, warm summer to a cold, wet winter: one day it's 90 and arid, the next it's 65 and pouring. Other times, it all comes in a single day. Soon, it will be one kind of thing for months. So, too, with natural boundaries: icebergs calve into the sea, shorelines form and erode, grasslands and boreal forests compete for space. It's where the earth is most rich with differences, and life throbs with possibilities.

In our own community, we are ankle deep in boundary moments, a continuous tension of moving out of a past and into a future. The thing with transitions is they are hard to navigate, especially for young people; these are new experiences, and so it can be emotional, confusing, a time of second-guessing, of simultaneously wishing for two opposites: I want to go, I want to stay. Our task as the adults in this community is to help our beautiful students through this portal of change. In mythic terms, we are guides at the threshold, mentors along the passage. They need us to be watchful, a sign among many of our zeal for this work.

And let's remember how wonderful, how blessed we are to be called to this work, so much so that only our best—our sacred, faithful, communal best—will do for the students in our care.

196

May 15 – 19, 2017

1 message   Sun, May 14, 2017 at 9:06 PM

"The thing which the teacher should be careful about in regard to writing is to teach how to hold the pen and how to place the paper. This is of great importance, because students who have not been trained in the beginning to hold their pens correctly will never write well."

St. John Baptist de La Salle
"Correctly Holding the Pen and Positioning the Paper"
Conduct of the Christian Schools

While De La Salle always kept his soul inclined to God, his mind was bolted to the practical. You know his holy writing: *they are a letter which Christ dictates to you, touch their hearts, save their souls*, and all those Lasallian exhortations. But first, train them to do something. This chapter on writing includes an article on how to sit at the desk, another on how to trim the quill, and still another on how to use blotting paper. No detail was insignificant.

On Monday we enter the last three weeks of school for the 2016-2017 school year. Seniors graduate in 26 days. Minds stray. Students struggle to *The best predictor of what students can do is what they have practiced in class.* hold a grade, or attain one, may grow discouraged as the complexity rises past a known strategy or practice. This is a good time to remind students, in classrooms and hallways and before work, that doing good work means first to have practiced well, for—as research often reminds us—the best predictor of what students can do is what they have practiced in class.

It may be simple. It may be that we assume the students know some basic skills: sit up in your chair, track the teacher (or discussion) with your eyes;

when someone speaks, be courteous by making eye contact. Let's not assume. In these last days before the school year ends, let's remind our students to do their best each class and each day. Tell students to sit up straight, to tuck in their shirts, to straighten their ties, keep their eyes forward ("I need your eyes on me"), track information in their books, start their homework before class ends, be ready for class so everyone can learn, and, well, you know the list. These last few weeks will be critical for many; let your zeal propel your instruction.

Let every child know that we believe in them, that we care for them, that we hope for them, and that their efforts will redound to their success if they do, in fact, sit up straight to their desk, hold their pen correctly, and follow the lesson.

Monday is May 15, the day in 1950 that St. John Baptist de La Salle was proclaimed Patron Saint of Teachers. Enjoy a heroic Monday and a purposeful, practical week.

May 29 – Jun 1, 2018

1 message   Sun, May 28, 2018 at 8:32 PM

"They are a letter which Jesus Christ dictates to you, which you write each day in their hearts, not with ink, but by the Spirit of the living God."

St. John Baptist de La Salle
Meditations for the Time of Retreat, 3.2

In the Student Review Team[64] we have been looking carefully at seniors who are quite near the precipice of doom, checking in to see that they are completing workdays in Work Study placements and assignments for course work. For some, the efforts of teachers and counselors, of administrators and parents all come to bear fruit in the last days of May and into early June. Getting everyone involved to keep our most at-risk students on track is what we must do. It's not practical. It can seem counterintuitive for us that so many people step in, goad, push, exhort, call, email, text, tutor, pigeonhole after school . . . when the student does not seem ready to do anything. Success can sometimes be a threat . . . and the closer to the threshold a student gets, the more the threat looms. And so we help.

This is a complex, dynamic, and fraught time of year. Our minds are inside two years, simultaneously completing this year and planning for the next one. Budgeting, Admissions, interviews for new hires, the Board preparing interviews for a new President and searching for a school site. Some days, I slurp a few drams of morning coffee at 7:00 and then— *blink!* —it's 4:30 and we're closing the building, sending students home.

---

[64] Weekly meeting of Administrators, Counseling, and Work Study leaders that tracks the status of the lowest performing students and reviews support plans.

In these frantic, jammed days of last things, of test retakes, of after-school tutoring, paper revisions, of preparing for exams, let's remember that we are God's conduit to our students' hearts.

Let's breathe deep, recall the good we do when we see our students. Each one.

Let's look into the eyes of our students, shake their hands, remind them of the good they do, exhort them to keep on going. We got you.

Moreover, let's look to one another to hold us accountable to the great good we are called upon to carry out—to touch the hearts of our tired, sometimes flustered, often lonely, beleaguered, but always beautiful students, each one waiting for us to speak his or her name.

Let's do our beautiful work.

May 13 – 17, 2019

1 message   Sun, May 12, 2019 at 7:36 PM

"Have you neglected some students because they were the slowest . . . shown favoritism toward other students because they were . . . naturally possessing more lovable qualities than others?"

St. John Baptist de La Salle
Meditations for the Time of Retreat, 14.1

I've read this line on and off over the last 35 years or so. I never liked thinking about it. Every time I read it, I'd usually wince, because, well, I have done these things.

The human inclination is so strong . . . one gravitates toward the pleasant, revels in students with a strong aptitude. However, working with students who learn differently, or who struggle to understand, or whose skills are undeveloped requires so much and being effective in those moments can be elusive. But it's our juice.

To De La Salle, these moments are steeped in Jesus' teaching: "I was hungry, and you fed me; I was thirsty, and you gave me drink; I was a stranger, and you made me welcome; naked, and you clothed me; sick, and you visited me; in prison, and you came to see me."[65] This idea emerges throughout De La Salle's writing and in the *Rule of the Brothers of the Christian Schools* . . . we are to "give special attention to those of [our] pupils who have greater difficulties at school, personal problems, or problems adjusting to family life or society"(Article 29).

As we near the end of the school year, these kinds of student issues show up more – the pressures of semester grades, or a summer without the

---

[65] Matthew 25:35-36

school, tends to surface these conditions in a student's life . . . and it's when our students most need our "special attention," what De La Salle often called *zeal*.

Bless you all for the zeal and grace you show in attending to our students most in need.

May 26 – 29, 2020
1 message   Sun, May 25, 2020 at 8:17 PM

"Seek out the children who are far from salvation."

St. John Baptist de La Salle

In 17th century Catholic France, "far from salvation" meant bringing young boys into the narrative of salvation history—God revealed in human history—"to instruct, to teach, to guide" so that the poor boys of Reims, France could "create a life according to the Christian spirit." De La Salle exhorted his young Brothers to act as "visible guardian angels," to see their teaching and communal life as if it were "God working in their lives." It was their own salvation, too.

Placing De La Salle's writing about the salvation of souls in modern day Portland elicits various reactions in our secular society and even here in our own school. Nevertheless, our stance as a Lasallian Catholic high school in the mission field of Portland is a statement about who we are and what we do . . . we possess a zeal for our school's academic and educational work, and we see our students and community through "the eyes of faith." To this day, our work opens doors for young people to "create a life according to the Christian spirit."

We are in the last days of our school's 19th year, two months into COVID protocols we're creating on the fly, helping students far from our Lasallian reach, and we find ourselves vexed by the distance of online learning. Nonetheless, we worked hard to shrink that distance, to be personal, to surround students with our capacity, and to remind them they are part of a community that loves them.

In these last days, let's be strong for our students.

May 17 – 21, 2021
1 message   Sun, May 16, 2021 at 8:46 PM

In the previous 14 months, staff learned to teach online in less than a week, devised new daily schedules, write Handbooks and Protocols for distance learning. At the new year, staff and teachers devised hybrid learning schedules that accounted for students and staff who fell ill.

"Love is never on surer ground than when it persists despite suffering and difficulties."

St. John Baptist de La Salle
Meditations for the Time of Retreat

What you do every day is an act of love, never more so than this year when every conceivable obstacle lay in your path.

You've had to learn to teach all over again, rethink the Work Study program entirely, interview 8th graders who appeared as small squares on your screen, practice soccer and volleyball and basketball with few athletes and each wearing a mask, counsel students and parents, tutor, coach, and serve meals. But you had your life outside of school, if such a thing were possible. Was it not so that school had spread into our homes as well . . . our own children's school melded with our school. It was both isolating and suffocating.

There were fires and the worst air quality on earth.[66]

Then lockdown kept on, tighter as the year wore on.

---

[66] *IQAir* publishes a daily World Air Quality Report ranking the cities with the highest concentration of pollutants. September 10-12, 2020, as forest fires raged across the West, Portland's air quality ranked as the worst on Earth.

Then snow and ice and power outages.

And then we returned with a hybrid schedule.

Calling what we do "school" seemed a stretch since we have been so physically distant from our students and from each other. How do we do our connected, loving Lasallian school . . . how do we hold together "a spirit of community" under the stresses and strains of this year?

Our students, too, moved through all this . . . some on their own, some caring for siblings as parents worked, some running the entire household. There are as many stories of "suffering and difficulty" as there are students in our school.

It's May, now, and our community persists. We are here, pressing on with our work, into the last weeks of this school year. In some ways, so close to the end, it seems the hardest parts are still ahead. According to our Founder, this is when our love demonstrates that we're on sure ground . . . safe, protected, at rest in a community.

Let's pay close attention to each other in these last three weeks of school.

May 8 – 12, 2023
1 message   Sun, May 7, 2023 at 8:48 PM

"The wheels on the bus go round and round,
Round and round, round and round;
The wheels on the bus go round and round,
All through the town"

Verna Hills, 1939

It's 33 feet long and has a turning radius of just under 26 feet. It's painted "glossy yellow" because the human eye picks it up instantaneously in the periphery. Unloaded, it weighs about seven tons.

And it seems to bring out the awe-shucks in us.

Driving home Thursday, I headed south on Cully, hoping to avoid the usual I-205 traffic. Up ahead, a yellow school bus stopped, its stop-arm flapped out, and flashing red lights pulsed on the stop-arm and the bus's every corner. Traffic halted in both directions. And we waited. From my angle, no one had stepped out. A moment later, a small boy, a 2nd or 3rd grader, backpack slung over his shoulder, stepped out from the front of the bus and walked across the street to a parent waiting to receive him.

My worries about traffic delays and rotten weather evaporated.

Driving to school Friday morning, westbound on Killingsworth, I pulled up behind a school bus stopped at 60th. Two blocks after our green light, brake lights cast a red hue across my car's hood and the stop-arm flashed out, and we all stopped. A solitary girl stood at the curb, summer-y pants tucked into blue rain boots, a puffy coat with a hood, and she's holding a large piece of paper with a ribbon. She steps up to the bus, pausing as the door flings open, the red lights blinking.

While waiting, I remember Thursday's little boy and my mind zoomed up, imagining this moment all throughout the Portland area and Salem and Tacoma and Eugene and Seattle, south to Sacramento and San Francisco and Los Angeles, and hundreds of smaller cities and towns up and down the West Coast, and earlier, each successive pickup-hour sweeping across the earlier time zones . . . hundreds of thousands of school buses picking up millions of children, and we're all waiting for them to get on and go to school.

Why am I telling you this?

While there's so much breakage wherever we look, we universally honor the school bus . . . and wait for the student to cross the street or take a seat, a cultural emblem of our social contract and the moral importance of our work . . . to honor the students in our care . . . and, when need be, to stop everything and make sure the student is on board or safely home.

This you do every day. Bless you all in your beautiful work.

May 28 – Jun 1, 2024

1 message   Sun, May 27, 2024 at 8:01 PM

"He always makes his way back home. Can't shake him."

Alyssa Frangipani
Director of Lasallian Youth Ministry (LYM)
On how De La Salle's banner always shows up

Our history of losing the banner goes back quite a few years. As graduation drew near, we'd ask, "Where's Jack?"

There's something slippery about that banner. After graduation, we'd roll it up and put it somewhere. The next year, we'd wonder about its location all over again: did we leave it at University of Portland? Is he in LYM? Is he in a closet? Edgar knows, right? He spent the 2018 - 2019 school year rolled up behind my office door, leaning against a bookcase where I stashed empty mailing tubes. And when we moved twice in 70 days over the summer of 2021, right away, we wondered where he went. Is he here or in the warehouse? The thought conjured the closing scene of *Indiana Jones* where the ark of the covenant is carefully rolled into the limitless chaos of a government storage facility.

"Where's Jack?"

It can be like that a lot of the time. Put him away, get on with the day's minutiae, and look for him another day. We get after our work . . . planning the semicolon lesson (It's important; it really is!), or tracking down accounts receivable for February and March, or looking for a ten-minute window to talk with the Principal about an obscure data set. Always, there's something else first.

At least now we actually do know where he is. On the daily, he presides over LYM. You can see him from the Commons staring out from underneath the "Leave to Serve" phrase of our school motto.

Of course, it's not the guy . . . it's the ethos of our community and our presence with students that's the thing . . . Knight Times assemblies, scavenger hunts, mock trials, service on St. La Salle Day, class prayer, retreats, juniors asking old guard teachers and staff about TV shows we watched in the 1960's, a SO in Academic Resource Center being tutored for a Geometry test, seniors on their last day wearing their college sweatshirts, the courtyard benches at lunch full of students on a warm day . . . all artifacts of our Lasallian lexicon.

Jack's banner and the De La Salle mosaics through-out the school remind us of the Lasallian ethos that permeates our everydayness, how fulfilling the mission of De La Salle North Catholic starts with the adult community—*our precious gem;* how our myriad expressions of faith fuel our zeal—*our dual charism;* and how those forces animate our relationship with students so that we can touch their hearts—*our greatest miracle.*

Bless you all in your beautiful work.

Reflecting on May's Lasallian Meme

"You have been called by God to this ministry, and you have been given the grace of teaching and the gift of exhortation for the sake of those entrusted to your responsibility. Use these gifts you have received with care and vigilance."

St. John Baptist de La Salle
Meditations for the Time of Retreat, 1.2

At Parmenie, De La Salle contemplates his life in education: opening schools, training teachers, building communities. Financial, civil, and ecclesial obstacles were always a dissonant hum; nevertheless, multiple issues arose at once, swamping the work, calling into question whether the Institute would hold together.

Choose a prompt to write about

> ➢ Consider this year, those opening weeks, your plans and restarts, your just-right steps and occasional missteps, the faces and your fit among colleagues, the growth and changes of your students. Write about one such moment when the forces and pressures were so steep that you wondered if your work was futile. What did you or your team do to keep going?
> ➢ Consider an issue or theme emerging for you this ninth, and last, month; then, write about it through this Lasallian meme of being called to the work, and the consequent sharpening of your grace and gifts to the ceaseless demands of the work. How did you or your team respond?

Epilogue
honorable lives

Epilogue

"What a joy it will be to see that your students received the word of God in your lessons . . . which will be apparent in the honorable lives they continue to live."

St. John Baptist de La Salle
Meditations for the Time of Retreat, 15.3

Your work and words remain with students, resurfacing intermittently through their lifetimes, a burst of your remembered face, a recollection of how you helped them in some way.

When this happens, they speak your name aloud to someone, and they tell a story about you—the moment they needed a teacher, and you were there.

You are part of their life story though you may never know or hear of it.

It's natural to wonder, *how will my students fare in the world?*

De La Salle's assertion, written as inspiration for a summer retreat, rings true for every educator. Your instruction helps your students grow in wisdom and grace, and then they go out in the world and live their honorable lives.

Jun 1 – 5, 2021
1 message   Sun, May 31, 2021 at 9:11 PM

"You carry out a work that requires you to touch hearts."

St. John Baptist de La Salle
Meditation 43:3

In his waning years, De La Salle wrote a letter to two benefactors noting the years of "trials and crosses" in establishing the Christian Schools, the many forms of opposition and the multiple trials he and the Brothers faced; and yet the founding took root, and schools throughout France flourished. Notwithstanding the differences between 17th century Reims and 21st century Portland, the spirit of De La Salle's meme holds up. Establishing our beloved school has not been without difficulties, but here we are.

There's a generation of young people out in the world, agents of deep good, because of the work you—and others before you—have held to. Up ahead, generations more still to come.

One need not look back very far to be impressed by your commitment and zeal. In March 2020, did you not, all of you, pivot in 48 hours from in-person to online instruction? As a community, you looked to each other to reinvent the work you had dedicated yourselves to. However difficult that was, you nonetheless took it on and kept the mission alive.

Amid the broadening crisis wrought by COVID-19, you have carried out De La Salle's greatest call to "touch the hearts of your students."

You have been, and most certainly will be, truly remarkable.

⊕   ⊕   ⊕

Fall 2025
A Message To Every Lasallian Community

"Union in a community is a precious gem, which is why Our Lord so often recommended it to his disciples before he died. If we lose this, we lose everything. Preserve it with care, therefore, if you want your community to survive."

St. John Baptist de La Salle
Meditation 91.2

As a Lasallian community, you understood your students and were able to guide them. Now, they're ready. Time to graduate.

We enter a contrived timelessness, an annual rite wherein we wear what we always wear, say what we always say, do what we always do, see what we always see. Music, processions, prayer, regalia, valedictories, awards.

The ceremony's sameness suspends time. It seems like all graduations before, and all those to come.

Finally, the heart of the moment arrives . . . diplomas . . . and the moment sheds its sameness.

The Lasallian call to serve originates in a Spirit of Faith, one's inner journey, an intimation of the divine, a heart disposed to transcendence and ready for the Lasallian mission: to provide a human and Christian education to the students confided to our care.

This, we cannot do alone.

That raucous celebration reverberating in the auditorium is the noisy outward sign of our community's inward grace, how we—in our idio-syncratic ways—taught the harder things: how to study, how to believe, how to trust, how to work hard, how to get back up after a loss, how to be a friend, how to be yourself when the broader culture urges you to be someone else.

As students' names are read aloud and they walk to the dais for their di-plomas, stories play cinematically in our minds . . . we remember the student as a FR stumped by an essay topic, a SO hunched over a desk staring at a dust mote, a JR vexed by polynomials, a SR despondent over a friend's betrayal while the prospect of leaving for college roils them every night. Zealous, we persist; faithful, we trust. In time, the story turns; our students grow in wisdom and grace. Now, here they are on the stage, holding a diploma, about to step into their adult lives.

This is why each graduation is a vital artifact of our Lasallian legacy.

These stories we tell each other—and well we should—are modern day epistles, emanations of the Spirit of Community, a reminder that we work in a spiritual field.

Let the year-of-memories resonate. It's always the year's arc of obsta-cles that tests the mettle of a community and burnishes the beautiful work.

Tell Your Lasallian Story

> "Union in a community is a precious gem, which is why Our Lord so often recommended it to his disciples before he died. If we lose this, we lose everything. Preserve it with care, therefore, if you want your community to survive."
>
> St. John Baptist de La Salle
> *Meditation 91.2*

The year is done. In Meditation 91, De La Salle asks the Brothers to contemplate three questions: How have you honored God? How have you acted toward your colleagues? How have you fulfilled your duties as an educator?

Choose a prompt to write about

➢ It's the storytelling that evinces a shared mission and purpose. What's the one story you tell people about a student or a colleague who brought out the best in you?

➢ Consider the sequence: God, Colleagues, Students. In what way has this sequence been foundational to your work this year?

➢ Despite difficulties, what has kept you in the work?

➢ In the 3rd movement of the 91st Meditation, De La Salle asks this question: "Did you apply yourself sufficiently to your teaching during the year?" To what extent does this describe your year? What might you do over the summer so that it remains true for the coming year?

➢ Write about a theme emerging for you at year's end; then, consider it through this Lasallian meme that "union in a community" is the source of your school's strength. How did you, your team, or colleagues work to preserve it or strengthen it?

"Those who have taught many people
to do what is right
will shine like stars for all eternity."

Daniel 12:3

The Beautiful Work

LASALLIAN SOURCES

If you wish to learn more about John Baptist de La Salle's life, there are three biographies which fulfill different levels of interests.

Start with Br. George Van Grieken's *The Teacher's Saint,* a compact read (2019, 98 pages) that provides a highlight overview of De La Salle's life work and influence. Next, Br. Luke Salm's *The Work Is Yours: The Life of Saint John Baptist de La Salle* (1996, 206 pages) contains updated research and reads more as a true biography rather than traditional hagiography. Finally, fulfilling a need for an authoritative biography that includes a deep historical context, Bernard Hours' *Jean-Baptiste De La Salle: A Mystic in Action* (2022, 626 pages) is a scholar's work, providing a rich historical backdrop coupled with analysis of multiple sources, opening new insights into De La Salle's life.

If, on the other hand, you want to know the man, read his three quite disparate books: *The Conduct of the Christian Schools, Meditations for the Time of Retreat,* and *The Letters of John Baptist de La Salle.* Here, you'll meet the school administrator, the spiritual guide, and the community director.

Aroz, Leon, FSC, Yves Poutet, FSC, and Jean Pungier, FSC. *Beginnings: De La Salle and his Brothers.* Translated and edited by Luke Salm, FSC. The Christian Brothers Conference, Romeoville, IL, 1980.

Blain, Jean-Baptiste. *The Life of John Baptist de La Salle, Founder of the Institute of the Brothers of the Christian Schools.* Translated by Richard Arnandez, FSC. Edited by Luke Salm, FSC. Volume 2, Book 1: Biographies of John Baptist de La Salle by His Contemporaries. Landover, MD: Lasallian Publications, 2000.

_____. *The Mind and Heart of John Baptist de La Salle.* Translated and annotated by Edwin Bannon, FSC. Edited by Augustine Loes, FSC.

Volume 2, Book Four: Biographies of John Baptist de La Salle by His Contemporaries. Landover, MD: Lasallian Publications, 2002.

Burkhard, Leo, FSC and Luke Salm, FSC. *Encounters: De La Salle at Parmanie*. Romeoville, IL: Christian Brothers Conference, 1983

De La Salle, Jean Baptist. *The Conduct of the Christian Schools*. Translation by F. de La Fountainerie and Richard Arnandez, FSC. Edited by William Mann, FSC. Volume 6 of Lasallian Resources: The Complete Works of John Baptist de La Salle. Landover, MD: Lasallian Publications, 1996.

_____. *Explanation of the Method of Interior Prayer*. Translated by Richard Arnandez, FSC. Edited and revised translation by David Mouton, FSC. Volume 5 of Lasallian Resources: the Complete Works of John Baptist de La Salle. Landover, MD: Christian Brothers Conference, 1995.

_____. *The Letters of John Baptist de La Salle*. Translated by Colman Molloy, FSC. Volume 1 of Lasallian Resources: Early Documents. Landover, MD: Christian Brothers Conference, 1988.

_____. *Meditations*. Translated by Richard Arnandez, FSC, and Augustine Loes, FSC. Edited by Augustine Loes, FSC. Volume 4 of Lasallian Resources: The Complete Works of John Baptist de La Salle. Landover, MD: Lasallian Publications, 1994.

_____. *Meditations for the Time of Retreat*. Translated by Augustine Loes, FSC. Edited by Miguel Campos, FSC. Winona, MN: St. Mary's College Press, 1975.

Hours, Bernard. *Jean-Baptiste de La Salle: A Mystic In Action*. Translated by Jean Fitzgerald. Washington, DC: Christian Brothers Conference,

2022.

Koch, Carl, Jeffrey Calligan, FSC, and Jeffrey Gros, FSC. *John Baptist de La Salle: the Spirituality of Christian Education.* Mahwah, NJ: Paulist Press. 2004.

Loes, Augustine, FSC. *The First De La Salle Brothers 1681 – 1719.* Vol 2 of Lasallian Resources: Early Documents. Landover, MD: Lasallian Publications, 1999.

Salm, Luke, FSC. *John Baptist de La Salle: the Formative Years.* Romeoville, IL: Lasallian Publications, 1989.

_____. *The Work Is Yours: the Life of Saint John Baptist de La Salle.* 2nd Ed. Landover, MD: Christian Brothers Conference, 1996.

Van Grieken, George, FSC. *The Teacher's Saint.* Washington, DC: Christian Brothers Conference, 2019.

_____. *Touching the Hearts of Students: Characteristics of Lasallian Schools.* Landover, MD: Christian Brothers Conference, 1999.

ACKNOWLEDGEMENTS

I am grateful for the spiritual and cultural heritage of the De La Salle Christian Brothers I experienced as a student at La Salle High School. I learned firsthand how preparing the hearts and minds of teachers redounds to the students in their care.

I am grateful . . .

To the Presidents and Principals under whom I served and who gave me the latitude to learn: Br. Tom Westburg, FSC, Tim Edwards, Bill George, Greg VanderZanden, Matt Powell, John Huelskamp, Tim Hennessy, Oscar Leong, and Ashleigh de Villiers.

To my generous early readers who helped me suss out a thoughtful organization while also providing valuable commentary and support: in particular, Leif Kehrwald, who suggested I frame all of it in a single school year; and Br. George Van Grieken, FSC, who accompanied me for the long publishing journey and steeled me to stay the course.

To a band of encouraging readers who offered sharp-eyed suggestions and buoyant morale boosts just when I needed them: Bonnie Ward, Ron Zaraza, Mike Daniels, Br. Mark Murphy, FSC, Charlie Legendre, Patti O'Mara, and Heather Ruple-Gilson. To Thomas Groome, Mary Fox, Susan Hines, and Tom Southard for their generous recommendations.

To 41 years of amazing colleagues who demonstrated, every day, how the hard work of running a school can be beautiful.

Finally—and exquisitely—to JoyFam . . . my bride Kim and our children, Megan, Ryan, Caitlin, Emma, and Hayley . . . who have loved and supported me through four decades of late nights, weekend obligations, and distant summer conferences. To the moon and back.

ABOUT THE AUTHOR

After attending St. Mary's College of California as a novice in the Christian Brothers, Tim returned to Portland, married, started a family, and finished studies at Portland State University and University of Portland. He went on to teach for 20 years at his alma mater La Salle High School in Milwaukie, a suburb of Portland, and then moved across town to De La Salle North Catholic High School, a startup school, where he served for 21 years as Vice Principal, Principal, and Director of Mission.

Now retired, Tim and his wife Kim live in Milwaukie, Oregon.

www.ingramcontent.com/pod-product-compliance
Lightning Source LLC
Chambersburg PA
CBHW021029130626
46552CB00005B/1758